AF633176

10 FUNDAMENTAL RULES OF SUCCESS

Compiler
Carani Narayana Rao, M.Sc (Ag.)

V&S PUBLISHERS

Published by

V&S PUBLISHERS

F-2/16, Ansari Road, Daryaganj, New Delhi-110002
☎ 011-23240026, 011-23240027 • *Fax* 011-23240028
Email info@vspublishers.com • *Website* www.vspublishers.com

Regional Office Hyderabad
5-1-707/1, Brij Bhawan (Beside Central Bank of India Lane)
Bank Street, Koti, Hyderabad - 500 095
☎ 040-24737290
E-mail vspublishershyd@gmail.com

Branch Office : Mumbai
Jaywant Industrial Estate, 2nd Floor–222, Tardeo Road
Opposite Sobo Central Mall, Mumbai – 400 034
☎ 022-23510736
E-mail: vspublishersmum@gmail.com

Follow us on

All books available at **www.vspublishers.com**

© Copyright: V&S PUBLISHERS
ISBN 978-93-813842-0-6
Edition 2017

The Copyright of this book, as well as all matter contained herein (including illustrations) rests with the Publisher. No person shall copy the name of the book, its title design, matter and illustrations in any form and in any language, totally or partially or in any form. Anybody doing so shall face legal action and will be responsible for damages.

Printed at Param Offseters Okhla New Delhi-110020

Dedication

To

My Guru, Shirdi Shri Sai,

My Mother, Shrimathi Carani Hamsa &

My Father, Late Carani Balakrishna Naidu

Acknowledgements

To

My Better-half, Ramaa,

Sons Nishanth, Mohnish,

Daughter-in-law, Kim and Grandson, Kishan

-for Their Love.

Thanks

To

The Various Writers In The Field Of Motivational Literature- For Motivating Me With Their Writings. This Title Is Possible Only On Account of Their Books On The Subject And The Compiler Is Indebted To Them All.

Contents

A word to the reader

"The ideas I stand for are not mine. I borrowed them from Socrates. I swiped them from Chesterfield. I stole them from Jesus. And I put them in a book." Dale Carnegie's comment, on his book, *'How to win friends and influence people'*.

I am an avid reader of books on self-improvement. It all started in 1960s with *How to win friends and influence people* by Dale Carnegie. Since then, I have read hundreds of self-help, management and business skills books. I observed that throughout the majority of the classics of self-improvement literature, there are 10 core rules to achieve success which run as a common thread. The purpose of this book is to share with you these proven principles/core rules/keys compiled from the vast success literature. These rules will definitely unlock the doors to success. Use these rules—these have helped me. These will help you too, to gain the winning edge in leading you from mediocrity to success.

In the following pages, **success** is first defined; then the rules involved in achieving success are enumerated and explained with relevant anecdotes and stories. Please read them and apply them to unlock your doors of potential. Your efforts will be well rewarded. I wish you all the success.

—Carani Narayana Rao

Success
(Achievement/Accomplishment/Attainment/Conquest/Triumph/Victory/Winning)

'You were born to succeed!
Success is Nature's law.'

What is success?

No two persons will define success in the same words; yet failure is always described but one way—Failure is man's inability to reach his goals in life, whatever they may be.

➤ *A survey among some American Executives asking them to describe what 'success' is, revealed responses falling into 4 groups.*

1] *For the first group, success meant owning material possessions, such as cars, buildings, gold, precious stones, etc.*

2] *For the second group, success meant experiencing particular feelings, like feel satisfied/happy.*

3] *For the third group, success meant achieving goals. They set goals, achieve them, and then set new goals. Here, success is a process of getting from one point to the next.*

4] *For the fourth group, success is related to their personal mission, hence, finding and fulfilling their mission will be success.*

The last group has deeper foundation than the first three groups which may run into serious problems such as material possessions which never satisfy for long; feelings are nebulous, and even goals can become meaningless after a while.

However, attainment of excellence in whatever field one chooses may be considered as success. The fields may vary—business, studies, politics, religion, spiritualism, research, management, governing, games, acting, singing, teaching, writing, social service, etc. Nonetheless, whoever has excelled in his/her field has an AMBITION and LIVES UP TO the FULFILLMENT of it. **Thus, we may consider the fulfillment of one's ambition as success.**

Success is not an accident

Success is not handed to anyone on a silver platter. No one just stumbles over a pot of gold or a good job, or lots of money or happiness. **Success must be earned.** The only way to earn it, is to utilize to the fullest extent possible, whatever combination of talent, skill and intelligence one possesses. Millions of people in this world, live a mediocre life with little or no ambition or fail to recognize/act on their true potential. Many of the people, who have plenty of ambitions, fail to attain their aim because, either they do not know how to achieve their purpose or they are not prepared to pay the price in sweat, sacrifice and sustained effort. The individuals who attain success will not only have ambitions but are also determined, diligent and persevering. Concentrating all their energies, they constantly strive hard for the fulfillment of their *ambitions,* with the optimal utilization of the available resources. Such accomplishments should be in line with the requirement of the society, good and useful. **Thus, success should be a progressive achievement of worthy and challenging goals or dreams.**

On our path to success, we have to fight the tendency to look at others and see how far they have come or to look for their approval of our success. *A thoroughbred horse never looks at other racehorses. It just concentrates on running the fastest race, it can run.* So, compete with yourself. **Your business in life is not to get ahead of other people, but to get ahead of yourself.** Your goal is to be better today than you were yesterday and to be better tomorrow than you are today. Strive for constant and never-ending improvement and always try to better your best.

Everybody wants success. But, the first and important step in achieving success is how you define success for yourself. People who don't have a personal definition for success, are less successful and are less satisfied with their careers and their lives. If you want to be successful, you must first define what success means to you. **Once you define success for yourself, then definite steps/keys are available to attain it.**

Success Formulae

Definite steps and keys to attract success

✓ To laugh often and much; To win the respect of intelligent people and the affection of children, to earn the appreciation of honest critics and endure the betrayal of false friends; to appreciate beauty, to find the best in others, to leave the world a bit better whether by a healthy child, a garden patch, or a redeemed social condition; to know even one life has breathed easier because you lived. This is to have succeeded.

✓ Success is being happy with what you have got. You can enjoy success simply by reaching a point where you are perfectly contented with your life.

Achievement is different from success. Achievement refers to 'getting what you want.' Achievement requires the ability to set goals and objectives, to make plans of action, and then to implement those plans, overcome obstacles and difficulties in reaching the goals that you have set.

✓ Getting something done is an *accomplishment;* getting something done right is an *achievement.*

✓ Don't confuse fame with success. *Madonna is one; Helen Keller is the other.*

✓ *Success is a journey, not a destination.* Success is the progressive achievement of worthy and challenging goals or dreams.

✓ A success is one who decided
to succeed________________________and **worked.**
A failure is one who decided
to succeed________________________and **wished.**
A decided failure is one who failed
to decide_________________________and **waited.**

✓ Every worthwhile accomplishment has a price tag attached to it. The question is always whether you are willing to pay the price to attain it—in hard work, sacrifice, patience, faith and endurance.

✓ **Four Ds of success:**

1] Desire,
2] Direction for one's desire/goal to achieve,
3] Determination and
4] Dedication of oneself to the act of achieving the desired goal.

✓ **A.S.K** for accomplishment and for expanding your comfort zone: Right proportion of—

1] Attitude that of a champion,
2] Skill from regular and rigorous practice and
3] Knowledge/intricate details of the resources/ inputs/facts and details/plan of the task to be accomplished or goal to be achieved.

✓ **Eight Ps/Four Steps for achievement:**

Plan Purposefully,
Prepare Prayerfully,
Proceed Positively and
Pursue Persistently.

✓ To succeed, one must possess an effective combination of ability, ambition, courage, drive, hard work, integrity and loyalty.

✓ **Formula for financial success**: Find a need and fulfil it.The man who will use his skill and constructive imagination to see how much he can give for a dollar, instead of how little he can give for a dollar, is bound to succeed.

✓ There is a four-word formula for success that applies equally well to organizations and individuals—'Make yourself more useful.'

✓ **Spell success:**

Select your goal.
Unlock your personal potential.
Commit yourself to your plan.
Chart your course.
Expect problems.
Stand firm on your commitment.
Surrender everything to God.

✓ **S** of success is for **superior relations**
U of success is for **unlimited energy**
C of success is for **creative thinking**

C of success is for **confidence**
E of success is for **effective communication**
S of success is for **self motivation**
S of success is for **superb memory**

✓ **S** of success is for **sense of direction**
U of success is for **understanding**
C of success is for **courage**
C of success is for **charity**
E of success is for **esteem**
S of success is for **self confidence**
S of success is for **self acceptance**

✓ It takes a little COURAGE
And a little SELF-CONTROL,
And some grim DETERMINATION,
If you want to reach a GOAL,
It takes a deal of STRIVING,
And a firm and stern set CHIN,
No matter what the BATTLE,
If you are really out TO WIN.

✓ **A.P.S.A.R.A**

Aim: You must have a definite aim and determination to achieve it.

Plan: Chart out a clear-cut plan to work for achievement of your aim.

Strive: Work hard, purposefully and systematically, until you achieve your goal.

Achieve: Never give up striving, whatever be the challenges and impediments.

Ruminate: Remove of all the ups and downs, joys and anguish, mistakes and brilliance that finally give you success.

Advance: Now move on to a greater and nobler aim. Repeat the process of Aim, Plan, Strive and Achieve.

✓ Success is the result of perfection, hard work, learning from failure, loyalty to those for whom you work and persistence.

✓ **DOPE** for success:

D- Determination (you are talented and capable),
Decision (on course of action) and
Discipline (to follow your schedule)

O- Observance (of rules and regulation),
Openness (enables you to listen to others to diffuse tensions) and
Offering (yourself to God in prayer and asking in faith)

P- Planning (takes you from where you are to where you want to be),
Patience (reduces your level of anger and arrogance) and
Perseverance (eventually pays rich dividends).

E- Exercise (at least for 30 minutes daily),
Excellence (means putting your best efforts) and
Enjoyment (necessary as it helps you to relax)

✓ *He worked by day and toiled by night.*
He gave up play with much delight.
Dry books, he read for new things to learn.
And forged ahead, success to earn.
He plodded on, with faith and pluck.
And when he won, they called it luck.

✓ List of qualities that contribute to success:

Ability – 5%
Knowledge – 5%
Discipline – 10%
Attitude – 40%
Enthusiasm – 40%

✓ **The ladder of success:**

0% – **I won't.**
10% – **I can't.**
20% – **I don't know how.**
30% – **I wish I could.**
40% – **I could.**
50% – **I think, I might.**
60% – **I might.**
70% – **I think, I can.**
80% – **I can.**
90% – **I will.**
100% – **I did.**

✓ There are two kinds of people on the road of life. Passengers and drivers.

✓ Winning is a habit, unfortunately, so is losing.

✓ **Napoleon Hill's list of twelve great riches of life:**

1. A positive mental attitude
2. Sound physical health
3. Harmony in human relationships
4. Freedom from fear
5. Hope of achievement
6. The capacity for faith
7. Willingness to share one's blessings
8. A labour of love
9. An open mind on all subjects
10. Self-discipline
11. The capacity to understand people
12. Financial security.

✓ **Albert Einstein's formula for success:**
If A= success, the formula is A= X+Y+Z with X being work, Y being play and Z, keeping your mouth shut.

✓ Often, the difference between a success and a failure is not one's better abilities or ideas, but the courage that one has to bet on his/her ideas, to take a calculated risk-and to act.

✓ ...People of accomplishment rarely sat back and let things happen to them. They went out and happen to things.

✓ **Winner versus loser**

Winner

- Is always part of the answer.
- Always has a program.
- Says, "Let me do it for you."
- Sees an answer for every problem.
- Says, "It may be difficult but it is possible."
- When he makes a mistake, he says, "I was wrong."
- Makes commitments.
- Has dreams.
- Says, "I must do something."
- Is part of the team.
- Sees the gain.
- Sees the possibilities.
- Believes in win-win.
- Sees the potential.
- Is like a thermostat.
- Chooses what he says.
- Uses hard arguments but soft words.
- Stands firm on values but compromises on petty things.
- Makes it happen.

Loser

- Is always part of the problem.
- Always has an excuse.
- Says, "That is not my job."

- Sees a problem for every answer.
- Says, " It may be possible but it is too difficult."
- When he makes a mistake, he says, "It was not my fault."
- Makes promises.
- Has schemes.
- Says, "Something must be done."
- Is apart from the team.
- Sees the pain.
- Sees the problems.
- Believes, for him to win, someone has to lose.
- Sees the past.
- Is like a thermometer.
- Says what he chooses.
- Uses soft arguments but hard words.
- Stands firm on petty things but compromises on values.
- Lets it happen.

1st Rule

GOALS (vision/definiteness of purpose/ aim/object/mission/target/destination/ aspiration/intents)

The law of *karma* or cause and effect

"For every cause, there is an effect, and for every effect, there is/are specific cause/causes. There are no accidents. What you sow, so you reap.

Definitiveness of purpose is the starting point of any achievement. You can have anything you want in life if you can first decide exactly what it is, and then do the things that others have done to achieve the same result."

Before you start out, you decide where you want to go. Would you sit in a train or bus without knowing where it was going? No. Then why do people go through life without having any destination or goal? *So, before you start out, know where you want to go.*

The law of clarity

"The clearer you are about what you want, and what you are willing to do to get it, the more likely it is that you will be lucky and get what you want. Clarity of desired goals is a magnet that draws good luck to you."

An individual objective is, the intended goal, which prescribes definite scope and suggests direction to efforts for better individual.

Goals give a direction to the enthusiasm and they point out to the end results. The world stands aside to let any one pass, who knows where she/he is going. Goals should be **S.M.A.R.T:**

- **Specific,** like "I want to become a *crorepathy.*"
- **Measurable,** like "I want to earn Rs 3 crore by the 50th year."
- **Action oriented,** there should be a plan and action is to be initiated.
- **Realistic,** If one wants to reduce weight from 80 kg to 60 kg within a month, it is not a practical one.
- **Time specific,** it must clearly be mentioned when the action is to be started and completed to achieve the goal.

List the things you want most in your life:

- Things you want right now,
- In the near future and
- Your final goal.

Write down on paper, your goals in life. If you keep your goals before you, each day, and act on them, they are certain to become a reality.

When you look for something, you will find it. If you constantly expect exceptional success, you will surely have it. Peak performers attract success. You must keep the goals, you desire to achieve at the forefront of your mind throughout the day. Repeat your ambitions at least five times a day, and visualize yourself achieving them. If your goal is to be rich, picture the house, you will be living in, the car you will be driving, what it will feel like to be rich and the pleasure of attaining your goals in life. Repeat your ambition over and over, until you have complete certainty that you will attain your desires and eventually, you will. Set goals. Do what it takes to achieve them, and enjoy your process.

The law of flexibility

"Be clear about your goals and be flexible about the process of achieving them. Flexibility and adaptability are the core qualities for success in an age of rapid change, competition and obsolescence."

Goal setting and pursuing one goal at a time are highly essential for success in one's endeavour.

➤ Goals - Plurality

A scholar had two sons. One was a priest and the other was a farmer.

One day, the farmer went to see his priest brother at his residence. A servant in the house said – "My master is busy. He is praying ***Lord Siva".***

The farmer said that he would wait outside and came out of the house. The farmer went out and started digging a pit.

After sometime, when the farmer enquired, the servant replied—"My master is still busy. Now, he is praying ***Lord Vishnu."***

The farmer started digging a second pit.

Again after sometime, when the farmer asked, the servant said that his master was praying to **Goddess Kali.** *The farmer dug yet another pit.*

This continued. Every time the servant announced that his master was praying to some God, the farmer dug a new pit.

At last, the priest finished his prayers and came out. The farmer rose and went to see him. The priest noticed the pits on the river bed and asked him – "What for did you dig so many pits"?

"For water", replied the farmer.

The priest laughed and said – "You fool! You could have got water by now, had you dug only one pit deep enough".

"You fool! You could have got salvation by now, had you prayed to only one God instead of many," replied the farmer brother.

2nd Rule

POSITIVE MENTAL ATTITUDE

(positive thinking/possibility thinking/ self-confidence/self-esteem/'can' ability/ optimism/faith/hope)

'That which any person who has walked this Earth has achieved, you can achieve with the **right mental attitude, perseverance** and **industry.** Limiting thoughts and weak mental images must be banished. One's focus must be on the attainment of goals that are truly important.'

The law of optimism

"A positive mental attitude is essential for success and happiness in every area of life. When you make a habit of looking for the good in every situation, you develop a positive mental attitude and eventually, you become unstoppable."

There is little difference in people, but that little difference makes a big difference. The little difference is in **attitude.** The big difference is whether it is **positive or negative.** So, in order to be a success, you need to cultivate a positive mental attitude. Your attitude is how you respond to the incidences/situations that occur in your life. Attitudes make a difference in success or failure. Attitude is a critical ingredient in the results that you will create in your life.

- *There was a giant who was bullying and harassing the people in a village. Nobody tried to protest him because of his gigantic size. One day, a 15-year-old shepherd boy came to visit the village and saw the harassment by the giant. Then he asked, "Why don't you stand up together and fight the giant?" They were terrified and expressed their doubt, "Don't you see he is too big to hit?" But the boy encouraged them by saying, "Don't you see he is too big to miss?" The villagers then killed the giant. 'Same giant, but different attitude.'*

Set a goal; *believe firmly and unflinchingly that you will attain it.*

Self-confidence *is the first requisite to great undertakings. Confidence begets confidence. If you have confidence in yourself, others will believe you.*

- **Heads or tails**

  A Japanese general decided to attack the enemy. The only problem was the number of soldiers he had under his command: One-tenth the number commanded by the enemy. Naturally, his men were not too eager to fight. He called his men and told them that he would toss a coin. If it came down heads, they would win. If tails, they would lose. He flipped the coin. It came down heads. Greatly encouraged, his soldiers then attacked the enemy and fought so well that they won.

His soldiers did not know that ***both the sides of the coin were heads!***

The dinosaur, the largest animal which ever lived, had never changed and therefore, became extinct. Make the decision to have a good, positive and productive attitude. It is in your hands.

Millions of people in this world live a mediocre life with little or no ambition or fail to recognize/act on their true potential. We don't realise what a wonderful piece of creation we are. We don't recognise our assets.

Life is not a game of chance. Life is what we make of it. Our life is the sum total of all our choices/ thoughts up to this present minute. **We can use our options, and choose what kind of life we want to lead – life of a winner or a loser.**

➤ *Once upon a time, there was an eagle's nest that sat on top of the highest mountain peak. A strong wind came and blew an egg out of the eagle's nest and it rolled down the mountain into a valley and ended up in a chicken farm. The mother hen hatched it along with its own eggs. The eagle chick which was raised along with the chicken by the hen, thought it was a chicken. It walked like a chicken, talked like a chicken, thought like a chicken and dreamed like a chicken. Chickens cannot fly, so it didn't even try.*

One day, while standing out, it saw the sight of an eagle flying majestically across the sky, like the king of the sky. The eaglet asked its mother hen, if it could soar like the bird in the sky. The mother hen replied, "We cannot fly."

The eagle could not take to flight and ultimately, died a chicken.

We are not to be chickens; we are born to be eagles to soar high. Know that we are eagles, let us flap our wings, fly like eagles and soar above the clouds. How? Before knowing the answer for how, let me ask you a question. Do you know which is the richest place in the world? Are they the gold and diamond mines of the African continent? No! The richest place in the world is the graveyard. Yes, the graveyard! In it lie all the people, who had great ideas, which would have made them wealthy and successful. Like the eaglet in the above story, they listened to some pessimistic person who dissuaded them with the word, *can't* which they believed. Then they took their great ideas along with the belief, *can't* to their graves. The world lost a chance to their best inventions/discoveries/songs/books/ideas/speeches. This is all because they listened to a pessimist's, *can't.*

- **The greatest general**

  A man died and met Saint Peter at the gates of heaven. Recognising the Saint's knowledge and wisdom, he wanted to ask him a question, "Saint Peter," he said, "I have been interested in military history for many years. Tell me, who was the greatest general of all times?"

  Peter quickly responded, "O, that is a simple question, it's that man right over there."

  The man looked where Peter was pointing and answered, "You must be mistaken. I knew that man on earth, and he was just a common labourer."

"That's right," Peter remarked, "But he would have been the greatest general of all time—if he had been a general."

Please do not make such a mistake of taking your riches with your grave depriving the world as well as yourselves of the great ideas.

So, cultivate a positive mental attitude. Be an 'Opti'.

➤ *Once, three frogs, 'Opti', 'Mathy' and 'Pessi' accidentally fell into a pail of milk.*

Pessi, *a pessimist, cursed life and his bad breaks. Pessi whined, complained, focused his energies on the problem and soon gave up and died.*

The second frog, ***Mathy,*** *a brilliant mathematician, figured that he could leap to safety if he properly calculated the distance. He computed the algebraic factors of the trajectory, worked out the parabolics and dynamics and then readied himself for the grand leap. Immersed in his cerebrations, he did not notice that the pail had a handle, and in his leap, 'Mathy' hit his head against it and lost his life.*

The third frog, ***Opti*** *had a different attitude—a positive perspective, a strong will to survive and love for hard work. He directed his energies to the solution rather to the problem. He kept on hopping and kicking. He did not give up. He kicked and kicked, until he churned the milk into cream, and then into butter. As it became solid, he eventually, leaped out to safety.*

Most people find what they look for. If they look for happiness, they get happiness. If they look for what is wrong with others and situations, they forget to see what is right.

➤ *A father and his two sons lived in a single room. The father used to come home drunk everyday and watch TV, disturbing his children's studies. The eldest son was committed and concentrated on his studies, while the younger son followed in the footsteps of his father. Both the children grew up. The eldest son got an award for being the best citizen in the town, while on the same day; the younger son was imprisoned for a petty crime.*

When both were interviewed, the answers they gave were worth pondering. The younger son said, "All because of my father, who created a bad atmosphere at home." The eldest son said, "I attribute my success to my drunken father and the unhappy home atmosphere; it was an inspiration for me to be different." The situation was the same but the response was different. More than the situation, it is how we respond to the situation that determines the quality of our life.

So, we need to focus only on the positive in life instead of looking for what is wrong. Remember, the overriding law of nature: Positive overcomes the negative.

Note: When you go looking for gold, you move tons of dirt to get an ounce of gold. But, you don't look for the dirt, you look only for gold. Focus on the donut, not on the hole.

- When a ship sails the high seas, water that can sink the ship is all around it. But, only that water which gets into the ship can sink a ship. Do not allow yourself to be influenced by the negative forces around you, lest it may sink you.

Many a times, we face problems in our lives that seem insurmountable or we have circumstances that we cannot change. But, look into the lives of the following, whose lives, despite having handicaps, have attained greatness. "When the going gets tough, the tough gets going."

- **Beethoven:** He became totally deaf. He ended up composing some of the greatest symphonies in this condition.
- **Charles Atlas:** He was teased, as a boy for his build. He ended up with a muscular physique that has been used as a replica for numerous famous statues in U.S.A.
- **Franklin D. Roosevelt:** He was confined to a wheel chair. He ended up as the president of United States.
- **Helen Keller:** She was blind and deaf from birth. She ended up becoming a famous writer.
- **Napoleon:** He was short. He ended up as a giant military conqueror.
- **J.Simpson:** When young, he had 'straw legs' (skinny) which were crippled with rickets. He ended up becoming one of the great running backs in the history of American professional football.

- **Socrates:** He had physical deformities, baldness and a "hefty physique." He ended up as one of the greatest philosophers of his time.
- **Winston Churchill:** He had a serious speech impediment. He ended up becoming a great leader and a forceful orator.

Never complain. Always be known as a positive, strong, energetic and enthusiastic person. Someone who complains, is cynical and always looks for the negative in everything, will scare people away and rarely will succeed at anything. From a purely psychological viewpoint, things are always created twice: Once in the mind and then in reality. Focus on the positive. Be so mentally tough that nothing takes you off your planned course to success. Visualize and firmly believe in what you want. It will most certainly come true.

We may suffer with certain fears. The eight basic fears are i] *fear of poverty,* ii] *fear of criticism,* iii] *fear of ill health,* iv] *fear of loss of love,* v] *fear of old age,* vi] *fear of loss of liberty,* vii] *fear of death* and viii) *fear of failure*. Don't try to flee from fear. We have to fight any fear with a positive faith. We fear most with that which never happens. We spoil our initiative by the fear of defeat/failure.

Associate only with positive, focused people who you can learn from and who will not drain your valuable energy with complaining and uninspiring attitudes. By developing relationships with those committed to constant improvement and the pursuit of the best that life has to offer, you will have plenty of company on your path to the top of whatever mountain you seek to climb.

3rd Rule

PURPOSEFUL-BURNING DESIRE

(magnificent obsession/enthusiasm/zeal/ intensified emotion/excitement/passion/ fervour/ambition/great drive/intense commitment)

The law of desire

"To attain success, you must have a burning desire. A mild desire or casual interest is not sufficient. You can tell how badly you want it by observing your actions each day. Are they consistent with attainment of success?"

The law of energy

"The greater the energy and enthusiasm you have, the more likely you will recognize and respond to luck."

You have a vehicle, say a motorcycle/car. You have chosen a destination to go. Now your vehicle can convey you to your destination. For your vehicle to move and reach the desired destination, fuel- 'petrol'/ 'diesel', is required. Though, the destination is chosen and the vehicle is available, yet without sufficient fuel, you cannot not reach the destination. So, also is with our life. If a goal is chosen and even if all the required resources/ inputs/facts and details required for attaining the desired goal are available, yet without the burning desire/intense commitment, the goal cannot be reached. When your goal becomes a magnificent obsession—whatever other qualities you need to reach the top will come to you. As the fuel propels the car, so also is the burning desire/intense commitment that propels us towards attaining the goal. ***Enthusiasm is the fuel of success,*** *hence, 'Enthusiasm' makes the difference.*

➤ **How intensive should be the desire?**

Narendranath (later he became a sanyasi and took the name Swami Vivekananda), a skeptic, once approached Saint Ramakrishna Paramahamsa asking him to show God. When they went to the river for taking bath, Ramakrishna Paramahamsa took the young man by surprise and holding Narendranath's head pushed him under water. Narendranath kicked, bit and clawed to get the hand off his head. At last, Ramakrishna Paramahamsa released him so that he could come up for a gasp of air. Ramakrishna Paramahamsa asked, "What did you want the most when you were under water?" Narendranath replied, "Air". Ramakrishna Paramahamsa said, "When you want God as badly as you wanted air, then surely you will find Him." Thus, Ramakrishna Paramahamsa practically showed Narendranath, the level of intensity, required to see God. Narendranath, subsequently as Swami Vivekananda, with all passion took up the message of Ramakrishna Paramahamsa to start Ramakrishna Mission, which now has branches all over the world. If God can be found applying such intensity, achieving any other desire with the same intensity can be just a cakewalk.

- *Another analogy is the 'Volcano'. Do you want to be unstoppable? Then, be a human 'Volcano'. When a mountain becomes a 'Volcano', it turns on, comes alive, lights up, radiates a glow and becomes a shaker and mover. Its source of power is Heat. Get Hot and Intensive, like a 'Volcano'. No one dares to oppose the oncoming, unstoppable, constantly spreading, all-consuming heat.*

Thus, the burning desire, a desire with emotional intensity, is the starting force for all achievements. A small fire cannot give much heat, so, also a weak desire cannot produce great results. The burning desire backed by unwavering commitment turns the impossible into possible.

- *After throwing him out of a train in the apartheid South Africa,* ***Mahatma Gandhi*** *developed the obsession to send the British away as well as to eradicate untouchability.*
- ***Thomas Alva Edison,*** *used to work in his laboratory non-stop, often for two to three days straight away, without sleep, because he was obsessed with inventing the light bulb.*
- *For several thousands of years, people held the belief that it was impossible for any human being to run a mile in less than 4 minutes. It is* ***Dr. Roger Bannister's*** *desire, to prove otherwise, which broke the four-minute mile for the first time on the 6th of May, 1954.*
- ***Karl Marx's*** *desire was to establish communism.*

4th Rule

Positive, practical & step-by-step **PLANNING & PREPARATION**

The law of planning and preparation

"Every minute spent in planning, saves ten minutes in execution.

List out everything that you can think of that you will need to do for the foreseeable future. Analyze your list and set clear your priorities. Discipline yourself not to work on small things, but to work only on those activities that have the most significant impact and influence on your life.

Luck is when opportunity meets preparation. Perfect performance comes from painstaking preparation, often for weeks, months and years in advance. The most successful people in every area invariably spend far more time in preparation, than the least successful."

After a goal is set, next we must evolve a **plan of action** in achieving it. Planning is the first step in any meaningful action. A plan of action is basically laying down activities involved in the execution of the task, arranging them in order of priorities and fixing up of a time frame for achieving the goal. Planning helps in better utilization of resources. Confidence comes from **preparation,** which is nothing but planning and practising. There is no substitute for preparation and practice, which give you the competitive edge. "If you give me ten minutes to chop down a tree, I will spend my first two minutes sharpening my axe."

5th Rule

RESOURCES (inputs/facts and details)

Nothing can come of nothing. There are many ingredients that go to make up success like, moments (time), men, materials, machines, methods, money, management, markets, mobility, facts, details, attitudes, skills, will, knowledge, etc. "Our charge on earth is to exercise our gifts and talents to the maximum—and to care for all the assets, God has given us, including our bodies." To be effective, you should always try to achieve your goals with minimum expense of moments (time), money and movement (mobility).

The law of maximization

"You always try to get the very most in exchange for your time, money, efforts or emotions. When given a choice between more or less for the same contribution, you will always choose more.

People are therefore, basically greedy in everything they do. This is neither good nor bad in itself. It just is."

The resources are dealt with, in detail under the following heads.

I. **Time and its management**:

a) Carpe Diem — SEIZE THE DAY!

b) Sleepless

c) *'To-do' list:*

d) Prioritize

e) Important but not immediate

f) Punctuality and promptness

g) Pareto principle/80/20 Rule — the Law of the 'trivial many' and the 'vital few'

h) Effective/efficient: Do the right thing (being effective) than to do things right (being efficient).

i) Procrastination and Success are diametric opposites.

j) Ask to get whatever you want

k) 'NO': Learn to say 'no' tactfully

l) Pursuit for Excellence: Strive for excellence, not for perfection.

m) Winning edge.

n) Timewasters

o) Relaxation time

II. **Health**

III. **Courage**

IV. **Strengths and weaknesses**

V. **Attitude**

VI. **Will** (to do) **and skill** (required for the job/work/ achieving the goals)

VII. **Enthusiasm**: Enthusiasm is the fuel of success

VIII. **Initiative**

IX. **Creativity/resourcefulness/ingenuity**

X. **Experience**

XI. **Appearance**

XII. **Orderliness and neatness**

XIII. **Courtesy, politeness and manners**

XIV. **Charisma**

XV. **Life**: Live life

XVI. **Have Luck!**

XVII. **Skills** (knowledge+practice)/**continuous learning**

a) Be eager to learn. Increase your knowledge

b) Improve your skills/Practice

c) Comfort zones

d) Decision making

e) Communication

f) Interpersonal skills

g) Negotiation skills

h) Selling skills

I. Time and its management

Time has power to change lives. At this point, it is worth quoting from ARNOLD BENNETT'S, "How to live on 24 hours a day"?

"The proverb that *time is money,* understates the case. Time is that inexplicable raw material of everything, without which, nothing is possible. The supply of time is a daily miracle. You wake up in the morning and lo! Your purse is magically filled with 24 hours of un-manufactured tissue of your life. It is yours. The most precious possession showered upon you in a manner as singular as the commodity itself.

For remark! No one can take it from you. It is un-stealable. And no one receives either more or less than you receive. Wealth or genius is never rewarded by even an extra hour a day. And there is no punishment. Waste this precious commodity as you will, and yet the supply will never be witheld from you.

You have to live on these 24 hours of daily time. Out of it, you have to spin health, pleasure, money, content, respect and the evolution of your immortal soul... But, if one cannot arrange that, an income of 24 hours a day shall exactly cover all properties of expenditure, one does muddle one's whole life definitely."

So, you have one thing in common with all successful people, a twenty-four hour day—it is how you use it that makes the difference. The one that uses it properly, prospers and the one that misuses it, fails. Time is the most mismanaged resource. Do you love life? Then do not squander time, for that is the stuff that life is made of. Time is the scarcest resource and unless it is managed nothing else can be managed. He, who cannot manage his time, cannot manage anything whatsoever.

The resource — **Time** is dealt with, in detail under the following heads.

a) ***Carpe Diem:*** Seize the Day!

Life is strange and so unpredictable. Some people are here one minute, and gone the next! Therefore, we should not only seize the day, but, also the moment – *Carpe Diem* and *Carpe Momentum.* **Do it now.** Later never comes, there is only now.

b) Sleep less

This is one of the best investments, you can make to make your life more productive and rewarding. Most people do not need more than 6 hours to maintain an excellent state of health. Try getting up one hour earlier for 21 days and it will develop into a powerful habit. Remember, it is the quality not the quantity of sleep that is important. And just imagine, having an extra 30 hours a month to spend on the things that are important to you.

c) 'To-do' list

Keep a list of things, to do everyday. This 'to-do' list will simplify your life. 'Put first things first', i.e., to prioritize your use of time, so that you focus on the important, high pay-off activity rather than activity that is a distraction.

- ✔ People who want to appear clever rely on memory. People who want to get things done make lists.

d) Prioritize

> **The law of priorities/time pressure** states that: "There is never enough time to do everything, but there is always enough time to do the most important things.

Your ability to set clear and accurate priorities on your time determines the entire quality of your life."

Make an inventory of the activities of everyday of your life. Reject all those activities, which do not suit your plan of life and retain only those activities, which fit in your plan.

Determine your priorities

By asking yourself the following **three 'R's,** you can determine your priorities:

1) What is **REQUIRED** of you?

2) What gives the highest **RETURN**?

3) What gives the greatest **REWARD**?

Focusing on priorities

Follow the **three 'E's** for focusing on priorities

1) **EVALUATE**—what is to be done.

2) **ELIMINATE**—superfluous tasks.

3) **ESTIMATE**—time frame to achieve the goal.

Six Ds: Work on hand can be sorted as under—

1) Don't do it: If that work, even if not done, is not going to put you to loss.

2) Delay it: If that work, even if delayed, is not going to put you to loss.

3) Deflect it: If that work, can be transferred to any other department.

4) Delegate it: If that work, can be delegated to any other person.

5) Do it imperfectly: After implementing the above, if the remaining tasks can be done partially, and if it is okay, please go ahead.

6) Do it: After allocating the work among the above 5Ds, what remain, are the ones which are to be done compulsorily and effectively.

You can assign a number to each activity in order of its importance. You can do a lot of activities, but do one at a time. Beginning immediately, start tackling the number-one priority on your *To-do list.* Stay on until it is finished. When it is done, cross it off your list and start on number two. Work down the list, crossing off activities when they are completed. At the end of the workday, prepare a new list for the next day. Transfer any uncompleted item to the new list and add on new assignments. Again, assign top priority to the most urgent task and so on down the list. Keep this up everyday. You will astonishingly be accomplishing so much everyday.

- *One day, an expert in time management was speaking to a group of business students and, to drive home a point, he used this illustration. As he stood in front of the group of high-powered overachievers, he said, "Okay, time for a quiz." Then, he pulled out a one-gallon wide-mouthed masonry jar and set it on the table in front of him. Next, he produced about a dozen fist-sized rocks and carefully placed them, one at a time, into the jar. When the jar was filled to the top and no more rocks would fit inside, he asked, "Is the jar full?" Everyone in the class said, "Yes." Then he said, "Really?"*

He reached under the table and pulled out a bucket of gravel in and shook the jar, causing 20 pieces of gravel to work themselves down into the space between the big rocks. Then, he asked the group once more, "Is the jar full?" By this time, the class was on to him. "Probably not". One of them answered. "Good!" He replied.

He reached under the table and brought out a bucket of sand. He started dumping the sand in the jar and it went into the spaces left between the rocks and the gravel. Once more, he asked the question, "Is the jar full?" "No!" The class shouted. Once again, he said, "Good".

Then, he grabbed a pitcher of water and began to pour it in until the jar was filled to the brim. Then, he looked at the class and asked, "What is the point of this illustration?"

One eager beaver raised his hand and said, "The point is, no matter how full your schedule is, if you try really hard, you can always fit some more things in it!" "No!" The speaker replied, "That's not the point."

The truth this illustration teaches us is, "If you don't put the big rocks in first, you'll never get them in at all." What are the "big rocks" in your life? Your children; your loved ones; your education; your dreams; a worthy cause; teaching or mentoring others; doing things which you love; time for yourself; your health; your mate (or significant other). Remember to put these Big Rocks in first, or you will never get them in at all. If you sweat about the little stuff (the gravel, sand and water) then you will fill your life with little things, you worry about that don't really matter, and you'll never have the real quality time you need to spend on the big important stuff.

So tonight, or in the morning, when you are reflecting on this short story, ask yourself this question: What are the "big rocks" in my life? Then put them in your jar first. **(Please refer also to: 'Pareto principle or 80/20 rule')**

The key to successful time management, is doing what you planned to do when you planned to do it. Keep your mind fully on the task at hand. Only then, will you achieve all your goals and have time for the things that matter most. Although, it is imperative to be flexible (a bow too tightly strung will soon break), following your planned schedule which requires no more than simple discipline.

e) Important but not immediate

Be ruthless with your time. Set aside a few minutes each morning to plan your day. Plan around your priorities and focus on not only those tasks which are immediate, but not important (i.e., many telephone calls) and especially, those which are important, but not urgent, for these allow for the greatest personal and professional development. Important but not immediate activities are those, which produce long-term, sustainable benefits and include exercise, strategic planning, the development of relationships and professional education. Never let the things which matter most, be placed in the backseat as compared to those that matter least.

f) Punctuality and promptness

Meeting appointments promptly saves yourself and others, both time and annoyance. Attending promptly to the things arranged in the order of importance, in the daily *To-do list* helps to keep the mechanics of life running smoothly. Thus, one gets the most value from time by using it according to a well-laid plan. Then one can manage work and other duties and still have time for recreation, social pleasures, etc.

Punctuality reflects professionalism in —

- Attending events
- Returning phone calls and e-mails
- Starting the workday
- Turning in proposals with deadlines.
- Unfaithfulness in keeping an appointment is an act of clear dishonesty. You might as well borrow a person's money as his time.

g) Pareto principle or 80/20 Rule

It suggests the **Law of the 'trivial many' and the 'vital few'.** Identify and concentrate on the minority of things (both positive and negative) that contribute most to achieving your goals. The 'important' things are those 20% of activities that offer us the big results. (In a classroom, 20% of the students will take up 80% of the teacher's time). There is never enough time to do everything, but there is always enough time to do the most important things. The art of being wise is the art of knowing what to overlook. Things which matter most, must never be at the mercy of things which matter least.

h) Effective/efficient

Be effective: Do the right things; focus on the end/ result to be achieved.

Be efficient: Do the things in the right way. Focus on means. **Faultless and speedy use of the means is the measure of efficiency.**

Efficiency, like rules and procedures, is relevant only to facilitate effectiveness. It is more important to do the right thing than to do things right.

Don't just be efficient. Be effective. To be the best, be both efficient and effective. Between the two, effectiveness is more important.

> **The law of forced efficiency:** "There is never enough time to do everything, but there is always enough time to do the most important things.
>
> The more you take on, the more efficient you become. You only learn how much you can actually do by trying to do too much."

Handle a piece of paper only once. There can be economy only where there is efficiency.

i) Procrastination and success

Procrastination and success are diametric opposites. Procrastination is self-destructive behaviour. Procrastination is the assassination of inspiration. Fear of failure, fear of imperfection and fear of inferiority are the procrastinator's greatest fears.

When you are procrastinating on a major task, slice it up into as many small, manageable 'instant tasks' as possible. Divide and conquer.

Don't put it off, for delay can be dangerous. **Tomorrow belongs to God** and **Today belongs to us.** Do it now.

- **Fear of failure**

  Sometimes, it is not criticism but fear of failure which paralyses a person.

  A mother had two sons as her only source of livelihood. Her first son sold umbrellas and the other sold fans.

  The mother could not help but worry about their business. When it was cold or cloudy, she would worry about her son selling fans. When it was nice and sunny, she would worry about her son selling umbrellas. No matter what the weather, there was still room for worry.

  One day, an old sage visited her village. In need of help, she went to this wise man. The learned man, after patiently hearing her story, said: "You are blessed. There is no way you can lose. If the sun is shining, people will buy fans; if it rains, people will buy umbrellas. Either way—you can't help but win."

  From that day, according to this folklore, the mother realised her mistakes and stopped worrying.

  Do something everyday that you don't want to do. This is the golden rule for acquiring the habit of doing your duty without pain.

j) Ask to get whatever you want

Ask to get whatever you want. It is a scientific finding of psychologists, that a favourable response to Asking is a 'conditioned response', developed in everybody starting in early childhood, continued constantly during all the years of schooling and established as the principal business procedure for getting things done. People cannot easily say 'no'. That is why people will do what you ask. Asking must be friendly, courteous, reasonable and persuasive—without offensive pressure and threatening argument.

> ➤ *Jack and Jill were walking from a religious service.*
>
> *Jack wonders whether it would be alright to smoke, while praying.*
>
> *Jill replies, "Why don't you ask the priest?"*
>
> *So, Jack goes up to the priest and asks, "Priest, may I smoke while I pray?"*
>
> *But the priest says, "No my son, you may not. That's utter disrespect to our religion."*
>
> *Jack goes back to his friend and tells him what the good priest told him.*
>
> *Jill says, "I am not surprised. You asked him the wrong question. Let me try".*
>
> *And so, Jill goes up to the priest and asks, "Priest, may I pray while I smoke?"*
>
> *To which the priest eagerly replies, "By all means, my son. By all means."*
>
> ***The reply you get* depends upon the question you ask!**

k) 'NO': Learn to say 'no' tactfully

You must say 'no' tactfully but firmly to the requests that do not contribute to the achievement of your goals. No one ever went broke by saying, 'no' too often.

Do not be too quick in saying, 'yes' and do not be too slow in saying, 'no'—the consequence will be your future.

Learn to say, 'no' tactfully, but firmly to the requests that do not contribute to the achievement of your goal or goals.

Rarely, you may get a negative response. Then you should be deaf to 'no' from others. In many cases it is not a decision. They want to get convinced. Never take for granted that you will be refused. People find it difficult to refuse a confident request. Some people like to be asked repeatedly and with coaxing to boost their importance. Make them feel important and you can get their acceptance.

l) Pursuit for excellence

"Excellence is an art won by training and habituation. We do not act rightly because we have virtue or excellence, but rather we have those because we have acted rightly. We are what we repeatedly do. Excellence, then, is not an act but a habit."

—Aristotle

> **The law of excellence:** "Excellent rewards are paid for excellent performance, excellent products or excellent service. The quality of your life will be determined by your commitment to excellence more than by any other factor."

Strive for excellence, not for perfection. Human beings can never be perfect, only God, our creator is perfect. Perfection (without fault or defect) is unattainable, frustrating and neurotic. Excellence (of high quality) is attainable, gratifying and healthy. **So don't be perfect, just be your best. That is excellence.** Then the work becomes an avenue of self expression and an expression from heart. Work also becomes enjoyment for when work is an enjoyment, it will not be drudgery. Steer your whole endeavour to touch EXCELLENCE. Excellence is self expression and harmony resulting in attaining peace as well as happiness and that is ultimately called 'success'.

Striving for excellence is progress. So, your level of performance is a choice. You can settle for mediocrity, or you can strive for excellence.

Efficiency is doing things right.

Effectiveness is doing right things.

Excellence is doing right things right.

➤ *In Texas, years ago, almost all of the oil came from surface operations. Then someone got the idea that there were greater sources of supply, deeper down. A well was drilled five thousand feet deep. The result? A gusher. Too many of us operate on the surface. We never go deep enough to find the supernatural resources. The result is, we never operate at our best. More time and investment is involved to go deep but a gusher will pay off.*

Better, make a commitment to excellence and always try to better your best. Excel in whatever you do. Then prosperity follows you.

Best of all rules

Work while you work, and play while you play,
That is the way, to be happy and gay!
Whatever you do, do with your might,
Things done by halves are never done right!
One thing at a time, and that done well
Is the best of all rules, as many can tell!
So, work while you work and play while you play.
That is the way, to be happy and gay!

The Gallup Organization in the USA, after extensively researching for twenty five years, has found the given common talents that are needed for excellence in hundreds of distinct roles.

m) **Winning edge**

The 'Winning Edge' concept says, "Small differences in ability can lead to enormous differences in results." Small differences in your own personal repertoire of knowledge can lead to major differences in your income and achievements.

Striving for excellence is progress, because there is nothing that cannot be done better or improved. All that we need is a little edge. The winning horse in the race wins 10 to 1. Is he 10 times faster than the other horses? Of course, not. He may only be faster by a fraction of second or by a nose, but the rewards are 10 times greater.

The same is true in our lives. Successful people are not 10 times smarter than the people who fail. They may be better by a nose, but the rewards are ten times bigger.

You don't need to improve 100% in any one area. All you need is to improve 1% in 100 different areas, which is a lot easier. That is the winning edge.

Talents	Sub-talents	Definitions
Striving talent	Achiever	A drive that is internal, constant and self-imposed.
	Belief	A need to orient your life around certain prevailing values.
	Competence	A need for expertise or mastery.
	Competition	A need to gauge your success comparatively.
	Desire	A need to claim significance through independence, excellence, risk and recognition.
	Ethics	A clear understanding of right and wrong which guides your actions.
	Kinaesthetic	A need to expend physical energy.
	Mission	A drive to put your beliefs into action.
	Service	A drive to be of service to others.
	Stamina	Capacity for physical endurance.
	Vision	A drive to paint value-based word pictures about the future.

Talents	Sub-talents	Definitions
Thinking Talents	Arranger	An ability to orchestrate.
	Business thinking	The financial application of the strategic thinking talent.
	Concept	An ability to develop a frame work by which to make sense of things.
	Creativity	An ability to break existing configurations in favour of more effective/appealing ones.
	Discipline	A need to impose stricture onto life and work.
	Focus	An ability to set goals and to use them everyday to guide actions.
	Formulation	An ability to find coherent patterns within incoherent data sets.
	Gestalt	A need to see order and accuracy.
	Numerical	An affinity for numbers.
	Performance orientation	A need to be objective and to measure performance.
	Problem solving	An ability to think things through, with incomplete data.
	Responsibility	A need to assume personal accountability for your work.
	Strategic thinking	An ability to play out alternative scenarios in the future.
	Work orientation	A need to mentally rehearse and review.

Talents	Sub-talents	Definitions
Relating Talents	Activator	An impatience to move others to action.
	Command	An ability to take charge.
	Courage	An ability to use emotion to overcome resistance.
	Developer	A need to invest in others and to derive satisfaction in so doing.
	Empathy	An ability to identify the feelings and perspectives of others.
	Individualised perception	An awareness of and attentiveness to individual differences.
	Interpersonal	An ability to purposely capitalize upon relationships.
	Multirelator	An ability to build an extensive network of acquaintances.
	Persuasion	An ability to persuade others logically.
	Positivity	A need to look on the bright side.
	Relator	A need to build bonds that last.
	Stimulator	An ability to create enthusiasm and drama.
	Team	A need to build feelings of mutual support.
	Woo	A need to obtain the approval of others.

Good, better, best
Never let it rest,
Until the good is better
And the better best.

n) Timewasters

Timewasters are lack of planning, lack of priorities, over commitment, management by crisis, haste, paperwork and reading, routine, visitors, telephone, meetings, indecision, lack of delegation, etc. Overcome them.

Following are the list of common timewasters encountered by majority of individuals.

Timewaster	Causes	Remedy
Lack of planning	Failure to see the benefit.	Recognize that **planning** takes time but ultimately saves time.
	Action orientation.	**Emphasise results** instead of activity.
Lack of priorities	Lack of goals and objectives.	List out goals and objectives. **Prioritise** them.
Over commitment	Failure to set priorities.	Put first things first.
Management by crisis	Lack of planning.	Recognize that planning takes time but ultimately saves time. Emphasise results instead of activity.
	Unrealistic time estimates.	Allow reasonable time. Allow time for interruptions.
	Problem orientation.	Be **opportunity oriented**.

Timewaster	Causes	Remedy
Haste	Impatience with detail.	Take time to **get it right**. Save the time of doing it over again.
	Responding to the urgent.	Distinguish between the URGENT and IMPORTANT.
	Lack of planning ahead.	Take time to **plan**. It repays itself many times over.
Paperwork and reading	Attempting too much in too little time.	Attempt less. Delegate more. Read selectively. Learn speed reading.
	Computer diarrhoea (flood of data/information from computer).	Manage computer data by EXCEPTION.
	Fail to screen papers.	Delegate reading to subordinates.
Routine	Lack of priorities.	Set and concentrate on goals. Delegate non-essentials.
	Over surveillance of subordinates.	Delegate. Look to results but not details or methods.
	Refusal to delegate.	It is impossible to get anything done through others without delegation.
Visitors	Enjoyment of socialising.	Do it elsewhere but not at workplace. Suggest lunch if necessary.
	Inability to say no.	Say no. Be unavailable.
Telephone	Lack of self discipline. Desire to be informed of and involved in all and trivial.	Screen calls. Be brief. Stay involved with essentials but not all. Manage by exception.

Timewaster	Causes	Remedy
Meetings	Indecision. Lack of responsibility for decision.	Make decisions, without meetings.
	Over communications.	Discourage unnecessary meetings. Convene only those essential.
	Poor leadership.	Use agendas for the meeting. Stick to the subject. Prepare concise minutes immediately after the meeting.
Indecision	Lack of confidence in the facts.	Improve fact finding and validating procedures.
	Insistence on all facts. Fear of the consequences of a mistake.	Accept risks as inevitable. Decide without all facts. Accept the right to be wrong. Use mistakes as a learning process.
	Lack of rational decision making process.	Obtain facts, set goals. Investigate alternatives and negative consequences. Make the decision and implement it.

o) Relaxation time

Schedule relaxation time into your week and be ruthless in protecting it. You would not schedule another activity into the time planned for an important meeting with the president of your company or your best client so why would you put off a period to invest in yourself? We must have time for ourselves to reflect, unwind and recharge our batteries. These are the renewal activities that allow us to maintain a peak performance and are exceptionally valuable periods.

II. Health

> **The law of energy:** "The greater the energy and enthusiasm you have, the more likely you will recognize and respond to luck."

Time without energy is no time. (I have right now a cousin who has all the time in the world—only he is in the hospital confined to bed). Energy is the product of good health.

Recall the wise saying that 'in a sound body rests a sound mind'. Never neglect the body which is intimately connected to the mind. This is your temple. Feed it with the finest fuels, exercise daily and care for it as you would your prized possession—because it is one.

Exercise regularly, watch your diet, eat healthy, take your vitamins, drink plenty of water, give up smoking and drink alcohol (if at all you drink) in moderation.

Keep your body fit. Make it a habit to exercise for at least 30 to 60 minutes, each day, to attain the **3 S: Strength, Suppleness and Stamina** in the body. Exercise can help you feel good.

Strength training: This involves exercises such as cycling, running, etc. for strong legs and arms. Start a program of weight lifting at the gym. Strong people are mentally tough people. As you age, you need not lose your physical or your mental strength. 75 year-old men are running marathons, 80 year-old women have scaled mountains and 90 year-old grandparents are living rich, productive lives. Whether you are 19 or 93, stay fit, stay motivated and stay passionate about life.

Do a hundred *sit ups* a day and do not break this habit. Strong abdominal muscles are very helpful to ensure that you enjoy peak health and injury free days. They also maintain your appearance and confidence level.

Suppleness (flexibility) training: Yoga, gymnastics, karate, etc. are some of the ways by which you can keep your body flexible. Peak performers are physically relaxed and mentally engaged.

To be at your performance peak mentally, your body must be loose physically and relaxed. It is now beyond dispute that there is a mind-body connection and when the body is supple, free from tension, the mind is clear, calm and focused as well. This is why yoga is such a beneficial activity. It keeps the body relaxed so that the mind can follow. Basic stretching for 15 minutes a day is also an excellent way to release tension that builds up as a result of our life in this highly complex and fast moving, but wonderful world. Try having a massage or power lounging in a Jacuzzi. Relax the body and the mind.

Exercise (aerobic) for stamina: Swimming, rowing, jogging, etc. for cardiovascular activity get the heart pumping more blood.

Cultivate the art of walking half an hour after you have finished eating your evening meal. Walks in natural settings are the very best. Walking is, perhaps, nature's ideal exercise. And when you walk, do not think about work or about the bills or about the challenges you might be facing. This will neutralize many of the benefits. Simply enjoy the walk. Notice the richness of your surroundings. Let your senses drink in the beauty of nature and the crispness of the air for a change. So many people who have mastered the art of growing younger, have also mastered the habit of a daily walk.

Try fasting one day every two weeks. During these fast days, drink fruit juice and eat fresh fruits only. You will feel more energetic, cleansed and alert. Fasting also has a salutary effect on your will power as you are subverting the otherwise pressing impulses in your mind calling on you to eat more.

Drown your appetite by drinking more water—ten glasses a day is ideal. It revitalizes the system and purifies the body. Also, get into the habit of eating soups and more complex carbohydrates such as rice, potatoes and pasta which feed your hunger with far less calories than other less healthy foods. You truly are what you eat and must ensure that your diet is designed to maximize your energy and mental clarity.

Remember: *No health, no energy. No energy, no accomplishments / no enjoyments.*

Peak performers are physically relaxed and mentally engaged.

III. Courage

"When you cannot make up your mind which of two evenly balanced courses of action you should take—choose the bolder," said W. J. Slim.

If you have a choice of taking two paths, always take the more daring of the two. Calculated risk taking often produces extraordinary results.

There is no substitute for courage and though the chance of stubbing your toe increases the more you walk, it is always better than going nowhere by standing still. Take chances, take smart risks and you will meet with success beyond your dreams.

> **The law of courage states that:** "Your willingness to risk failure is the only real measure of your desire to be successful/rich, but analyze and minimize risk in the pursuit of success.

The systematic, deliberate development of courage is essential to the achievement of success.

Fear is the greatest single obstacle to achievement.

Make a habit of always confronting the things you fear and doing them anyway."

Act tough and you will be tough. Have courage and inspire others with your actions. But always be considerate. Fortune and love befriend the bold. No guts, no glory. Most failures are not due to lack of Luck, but due to lack of Pluck. Life shrinks or expands in proportion to one's courage. Courage means the willingness to take risks, to accept challenges. Nothing positive happens, until you take full responsibility for your thoughts and action. *Positive people take responsibility for their own lives, where as unsuccessful people duck responsibilities.*

- *A person holding a butterfly in his fist asked Mullah Nasiruddin, "Tell me whether the butterfly is alive or dead?"*

  Mullah smiling cryptically replied, "How can I say that? The butterfly is in your hand. It is up to you whether you want to keep the butterfly alive or kill it."

Responsibility is like a butterfly. It is your choice whether you take it or leave it.

IV. Strengths and weaknesses

List your strengths and weaknesses. Count your blessings. Focus on your strengths and make better use of them. Get rid of your weaknesses.

V. Attitude

Be **positive.** Things don't change. You change your way of looking, that's all. The meaning of things lies not in the things, but in your attitude towards them. (Vide 2nd Rule).

- ***The market for shoes:*** *A shoe company wanted to expand its business to a country in Africa. In order to assess the level of demand for their shoes in that country, the director of the company deputed two separate teams there.*

  After a study of two months, one team sent a report that there was no market for shoes in that country as no one wore shoes.

  The other team concluded that the place had a great market potential because no one wore shoes.

Attitude is an anchor to soul, stimulus to action and incentive to achievement. Things don't change. You change your way of looking. That's all. The meaning of things lies not in the things, but in your attitude towards them. We don't see things as they are; we see things as we are. Attitude, more than aptitude, will determine our altitude. You've either got a good attitude or a bad one. The choice is up to you.

> **The law of happiness states that:** "The quality of your life is determined by how you feel at any given moment/event. How you feel is determined by how you interpret what is happening around you, not by the events themselves."

No one can insult or hurt you without your permission. One of the golden keys to happiness and great success, is the way you interpret events which unfold before you. Highly successful people are master interpreters. People who have attained greatness have an ability which they have developed to interpret negative or dis-empowering events as positive challenges, which will assist them in growing and moving even farther up the ladder of success. There are no negative experiences, only experiences which aid in your development and toughen your character, so that you may soar to new heights. There are no failures, only lessons.

Ability is what you are capable of doing. **Motivation** determines what you do and **Attitude** determines how well you do it.

R.E.C.A.S.T your attitudes:

- **R**ediscover yourself, people and situations around you for the strengths/talents/ opportunities.
- **E**xert to learn and develop.
- **C**ompete only with yourself, so that you try to be better today than what you were yesterday.
- **A**ppreciate others for all the good things that happen to you through them.
- **S**top complaining and be a part of the solution, but not of the problem.
- **T**ake time to plan and organize the daily routine.

VI. Will (to do) and skill

Will and skill are the two sides of the same coin. 'Will to do' alone, is of no use, if skill to do that particular task is not available. 'Skill' alone will not be of any value, if the person does not have the 'will' to do that task. Accomplishment of a task requires of a person, both the will and the skill to do that particular task.

- **Will and skill:** *A boatman painted his oars with the words, Will and Skill. When he was asked for the reason, he replied by taking hold of the first oar marked, and pulling on it. "You see," he explained, "when I use only Will, the boat spins round in circle and we make no progress at all." Then, he took hold of the second oar marked Skill and pulled on that. "The same result", he remarked. He finally, took one oar in each hand and got into a steady pull. "Will (to work) and Skill (required for the job/work) must pull* *together," he added with a smile as the boat shot rapidly across the stream.*

VII. Enthusiasm

Enthusiasm is the fuel of success. (Vide 3rd Rule).

VIII. Initiative

There are two kinds of people: Those who don't do what they are told, and those who do only that. **The secret of getting ahead is getting started.** Once you **get going,** the **going gets easier.**

Initiative is the quality that impels us to do that which ought to be done. Initiative is doing the right thing without being told. A journey of a thousand miles begins with the first step. No one admires a person who always has to be told what to do and prodded into doing it.

IX. Creativity/Resourcefulness/Ingenuity

> **The law of creativity:** "Whatever your mind can conceive and believe, it can achieve. Every advance in your life begins with an idea of some kind, and since your ability to generate new ideas is unlimited, your future can be unlimited as well."

Moments of expansion of the mind have led to the greatest ideas/discoveries of man throughout the ages. *Expansion of mind is that state when one begins to perceive a different dimension in relation to one's existence, which until that time remains concealed.* Though all see apples falling off trees, yet it took a

Newton to realize the law of gravity. It is a split second when the consciousness takes an evolutionary leap from the instinctive to the intelligent and intuitive plane. Expansion of mind can occur naturally in anyone and at anytime. But by practice, this state can be achieved.

- **The contribution:** *There was a wise king who had three sons. He wanted the wisest and the ablest to be the king. So he decided to test his three sons. He told each one of them to fill the old palace with something and gave them one gold coin each.*

  The first son thought that his father had gone mad. How could he fill the whole palace with something with such a small amount? So he squandered the money on booze.

  The second son thought that garbage was the cheapest thing available for the given amount, so he filled the palace with garbage.

  The third son pondered over and applied ***lateral/divergent/out of the box thinking*** *to do something special. He bought and lighted candles & incense sticks and filled the whole palace with light and fragrance.*

Think up ideas. Ideas control the world. Every idea is the beginning of a reality. Your own ideas will determine your success. The person who produces a constant flow of ideas for improvement is indispensable. He/she will never be replaced by automation or computers.

> **The law of innovation:** "Business breakthroughs come from finding faster, cheaper, easier ways to perform a task."

Generate ideas—to improve products/methods/ yourself; to reduce costs; to increase sales/productivity/ profits, etc. Combine, refine, modify, and clarify your ideas so that they will be more useful.

- *An Indian farmer died leaving behind 17 cows for his three sons. The will advised the eldest to take one-half, the middle one to take one-third and the youngest to take one-ninth. Since there were 17 cows, they were having problems in dividing.*

  One day, an old uncle heard about this dispute. He decided to come with his cow and do what was needed. Their uncle added his cow to the 17, making it 18. The eldest landed up getting one-half or nine cows; the second, one-third or six cows and the youngest one-ninth or two cows. Having given away 9+6+2=17 cows, he walked away with his cow. He had done what was necessary.

X. Experience

Whether good or bad, is an asset. *Experience is what you get, when you don't get what you want.*

XI. Appearance

Without attractive packaging, no product can successfully compete. What others see is your appearance/ how you look. "Apparel often proclaims the man," said Shakespeare. The power of dress is very great in commanding respect. Good clothes open all the doors. Be careful with your clothing and grooming and look like the kind of person who deserves respect, attention and special consideration.

There is no second chance to make a first impression in situations like an interview, a business meeting, a first meeting, etc. The first impression is often made by the dress, the facial expression and the first few words you speak. By dressing well, we show respect to the people we meet in any transaction and telling them that we take the transaction/job on hand seriously.

In terms of business attire, dark suits reflect power, sophistication and authority.

XII. Orderliness and neatness

It is the habit of being reasonably methodical, systematic and tidy. It is the habit of having a proper place for everything keeping everything in its place. Orderliness and neatness practised with reason make life more comfortable, efficient and gracious. A neat personal appearance makes people like us. Orderliness makes for convenience, when looking for something. *Order is heaven's first law for God does not roll dice.*

Orderliness and neatness show your tidy mind and your seriousness in the job/business on hand.

XIII. Courtesy, politeness and manners

Courtesy is consideration for the comforts and convenience of others. Politeness and manners are the practice of special little customs which have become traditional. Manners without courtesy are insincere and empty. Courtesy without manners is sincere and kind, but clumsy. The three together are like a good oil in the social machinery. They make things run smoothly and pleasantly. All doors open to **courtesy**.

XIV. Charisma

Charisma is a personal magic or charm, which arouses unusual devotion from others. A person, who has it, attracts a special kind of personal loyalty and enthusiasm.

The following are the ten qualities of a charismatic leader:

1. Be committed to what you are doing.
2. Look like a winner and act like one.
3. Have big dreams, a vision and reach for the sky.
4. Steadily advance in the direction of your goals.
5. Prepare and work hard at every task you do.
6. Build a mystique around yourself.
7. Be interested in others and show kindness.
8. Have a strong sense of humour.
9. Be known for the strength of your character.
10. Have grace under pressure. (John F. Kennedy said that, "The elusive half-step between middle management and true leadership is grace under pressure.")

Develop that elusive quality known as 'charisma.'

XV. Live Life

> **The law of accumulation:** "A great life is an accumulation of thousands of efforts and sacrifices unseen by others."

➤ *Success is more than the achievement of an ambition. A man, who could not afford chicken, determined to forego all leisure, pastimes and enjoyment in order to spend every moment on amassing wealth. His aim was to be rich enough to afford eating chicken for supper every night. When he finally became that rich, he had no appetite for chicken and no teeth to chew it.*

Life is as simple or as difficult as you make it out to be. Live life and use up all your years. Don't let life leave you! *Prepare your plan of life in such a way that it allows you to enjoy the short-term successes, while you proceed to win your long-term objective.*

➤ **Life explained**

On the first day, God created the dog. God said, "Sit all day by the door of your house and bark at anyone who comes in or walks past. I will give you a life span of twenty years."

The dog said, "That's too long to be barking. Give me ten years and I'll give you back the other ten." So God agreed.

On the second day, God created the monkey. God said, "Entertain people, do monkey tricks, make them laugh and I'll give you a twenty-year life span."

The monkey said, "How boring, monkey tricks for twenty years? I don't think so. The dog gave you back ten, so that's what I'll do too, okay?" And God agreed.

On the third day, God created the cow. God said, "You must go to the field with the farmer all day long and suffer under the sun, have calves and give milk to support the farmer. I will give you a life span of sixty years." The cow said, "That's kind of a tough life you want me to live for sixty years. Let me have twenty and I'll give back the other forty." And God agreed again.

On the fourth day, God created man. God said, "Eat, sleep, play, marry and enjoy your life. I'll give you twenty years." Man said, "What? Only twenty years! Tell you what, I'll take my twenty, and the forty the cow gave back and the ten the monkey gave back and the ten the dog gave back, that makes eighty, okay?" "Okay," said God, "You've got a deal."

So, that is why the first twenty years we eat, sleep, play, and enjoy ourselves; for the next forty years, we slave in the sun to support our family; for the next ten years, we do monkey tricks to entertain our grandchildren; and for the last ten years, we sit on the front porch and bark at everyone.

Life has now been explained to you!

Stephen Hawking, one of the great modern physicists of the world, is reported to have said that we are on a minor planet of a very average star located within the outer limits of one of a hundred thousand million galaxies. Are your problems really significant in light of this? You walk on this Earth for but a short time. Why not become devoted to having only a wonderful experience? Why not dedicate yourself to leaving a powerful legacy to the world? Sit down now and write out a list of all that you have in your life. Start first with your health or your family – the things we often take for granted. Put down the country we live in and the food we eat. Do not stop, until you have written down fifty items. Once every few days, go through this list—you will be uplifted and recognize the richness of your existence.

Ask not what this world can do for you but, rather, what you can do for this world. Make service an important goal in your life. It is a most fulfilling investment of time. Remember, in the twilight of your life, when all is said and done, the quality of your life boils down to the quality of your contribution to others. Leave a rich legacy for those around you to savour.

Two of the fundamentals for a happy, joyful life are balance and moderation. **One must maintain a balance of all activities and do nothing to extremes.**

XVI. Have Luck!

Why does luck smile at some while laughs at others? A psychologist—Professor Wiseman says, he has discovered the answer.

"Ten years ago, I set out to examine luck. I wanted to know why some people are always in the right places at the right time, while others, consistently experience ill fortune. I placed advertisements in the national newspapers asking for people who felt consistently lucky or unlucky, to contact me. Hundreds of extraordinary men and women volunteered for my research. Over the years, I have interviewed them, monitored their lives and had them take part in experiments.

The results revealed that although these people have almost no insight into the causes of their luck, their thoughts and behaviour are responsible for their good and bad fortune. ....."

Here are Professor Wiseman's four top tips for becoming lucky:

1. Listen to your gut instincts – they are normally right.
2. Be open to new experiments and breaking your normal routine.
3. Spend a few moments each day remembering things that went well.
4. Visualize yourself being lucky before an important meeting or telephone call. Luck is very often self-fulfilling prophecy.

Luck is when opportunity meets preparation. Perfect performance comes from painstaking preparation, often for weeks, months and years in advance. The most successful people in every area invariably spend far more time in preparation than the least successful.

XVII. Skills *(knowledge + practice)*/***Continuous Learning***

Success does not come from acquiring, achieving or advancing. It comes as a result of growing. It is right to be content with what you have, but not with what you are. So, make it your goal to grow a little every day.

a) Be eager to learn

Increase your knowledge, for knowledge begets confidence. Read widely and wisely as books develop your personality and strengthen your self-confidence. The real purpose of reading is not to accumulate knowledge but to use it. It is one of the key reason for obtaining new understandings and better ways to do things.

b) **Improve your skills/practice**

Any activity, skill or profession—law, engineering, medicine, cooking or whatever – no matter how well studied, collides at last with the acid test: Can one *do* it? And that doing comes from actually doing it. Doing requires Practice. Movie stunt men, who don't practise, get hurt. So do housewives. **One's skill and dexterity must be brought up to match the speed of the age one lives in.** That is done with Practice. 'Talent' is actually just practice. PRACTICE bridges the gap between "good enough" **professional skill** and **dexterity.**

There is considerable joy in **skill, dexterity** and **speed.** It can only be done safely with practice. Trying to live in a high-speed world with low-speed people is not very safe.

Chance favours the skilled mind. You have to be an expert in your field. The only way you can deserve success is to be more useful. If you are useful in many things, you will receive many successes, and the more indispensable you will be.

> **The law of practice:** "Practice is the price of mastery. Whatever you practice over and over becomes a new habit of thought and performance. Growth and fulfillment come from abandoning old practices and embracing new ones.

> You can develop the attitudes, abilities and qualities of happiness and success by repeating them until they are firmly entrenched as part of your personality.

Continuous practice of a key skill reduces the time required to perform the task and increases the output achieved."

c) Comfort zones

In the heating and air conditioning trade, the point on the thermostat in which neither heating nor cooling must operate around 72 degrees—is called the 'Comfort Zone.' It's also known as the 'Dead Zone.'

Comfort zones are comfortable ways of doing things. They are your personal areas of thoughts and actions within which you feel normal/comfortable/ at ease/unstressed. They include how you deal with people, use your time, talk, do a job, etc. Any of those, once difficult or fearful things that you now find normal or easy to do, are due to your comfort zone. For example, if you are placed in an uncomfortable situation such as public speaking, stress can turn on resulting in your trying to avoid the situation and to get back to your non-public speaking comfort zone. This is because you don't consciously seek discomfort and you would rather get back to the comfortable way of doing things. This usually happens with when you want to bring in change or try to be different from your normal self, change habit patterns, use new skills etc. But if you stick with the new and sustain the change despite the early discomfort, you get used to it and your comfort zone expands. 'Stick with it' is the key. Comfort zones are most often expanded through discomfort. Move outside your comfort zone and find adventure, excitement and new levels of satisfaction. Stretch your comfort zones by trying something new. 'Fear is the energy to do your best in a new situation.' Right proportion of

i) Attitude (that of a champion),

ii) Skill (from regular and rigorous practice) and

iii) Knowledge/intricate details of the resources/ inputs/facts and details/plan is required to expand the comfort zone.

d) Decision making

> **The law of decision:** "Decisiveness is the vital quality of all successful people. Every great leap forward in your life comes after you have made a clear decision of some kind."

Any management process, including self-management, is nothing but **deciding and communicating.** Deciding involves what to do (goals), how to do (procedures), who to do (assignment of responsibility), where to do (organising) and what corrections to apply (controlling).

> **The law of choice:** "Your life/where you are and what you are is because of all your choices and decisions in life up to this present minute. Since you are always free to choose what you think about, you are in complete control of your life and everything that happens to you. Even taking no action is a choice."

e) **Communication**

> **The law of communications:** "The quality of your relationships will be determined by the quality and quantity of your communication with other people."

Always remember the key principle that the quality of your life is the quality of your communication. This means, the way you communicate with others and, more importantly, the way you communicate with yourself. What you focus on is what you get. If you look for the positive, this is what you get. This is a fundamental 'Law of Nature.'

Communication is perfect and complete, when the meaning meant to be conveyed is the same, as the meaning understood.

➤ *A busy blacksmith was one day annoyed by the presence of the village nitwit. So, he tried to frighten him away by holding a red-hot piece of iron near his face.*

The simpleton smiled. "If you will give me fifty paisa coin, I'll lick it", he said calmly.

The blacksmith, eager to make a fool of the boy, at once handed him a fifty paisa coin and stretching out the red-hot iron, said, "Go ahead and lick it!"

To the astonishment of the blacksmith and the merriment of the bystanders, the boy ignored the red-hot iron. Instead, he held the coin up and slowly licked it. Then he hurried away merrily. To the blacksmith, 'It'—was a red-hot piece of iron, and to the boy, 'It'—was a fifty paisa coin.

One should take care to communicate in the receiver's language. Communication is a very important skill aiding in attaining success. Communication facilitates the decisions to be carried out. Persuading others requires very effective communication skills. Hence, effective communicators become leaders. Otherwise, communication gaps and misunderstanding will occur. Even silence, sometimes is a very effective communication.

A good written communication should have the 7 'Cs':

1. **C**ompleteness : Stating all essential facts.
2. **C**ourtesy : Pleasantly worded.
3. **C**onsideration : For readers' interest and level of understanding.
4. **C**larity : Using familiar/simple words, short sentences, avoiding technical jargon.
5. **C**onciseness : Avoiding superfluous and redundant expressions.
6. **C**oncreteness : Saying directly, leaving little room to imagine.
7. **C**orrectness : With numbers, dates and references.

You don't speak English, you speak American.

In the USA ....

U don't open conversation (on telephone) with a Hello but with a 'Hi'.

The telephone is never 'engaged', it's always 'busy'.

U don't 'disconnect' a phone, U simply 'hang-up'.

U never 'mess-up' things, U only 'screw them up'.

U never have a 'residence' tel. no., U have a 'home' no.

U never have an 'office' tel. no., U have a 'work' no.

U don't stop at the 'signals', but halt at the 'lights'.

U don't 'accelerate', U 'step on the gas'.

Your tyre never 'punctures', U may have a 'flat'.

The trains have 'coaches' or 'boggies', no more! but 'carriages' or 'boxes'.

There are no 'petrol pumps', but 'gas stations'.

'I don't know nothing', 2 negatives don't make a positive here.

U no longer meet a 'wonderful' person, U meet a 'cool' guy.

U don't pull the switch down to light a bulb, rather flick it up.

U don't 'turn on the heat', U 'turn on the juice'.

There's no 'Business Area' ... only 'business districts', and no 'districts' but 'counties'.

No one stays 'a stone's throw away', rather 'a few blocks away'.

There's no 'Town Side', it's 'Down Town'.

In hotel U no longer ask for 'bill' and pay by 'cheque', rather ask for 'check' and pay with 'bill's (dollar)'.

There are no 'soft drinks', only 'sodas'.

Life's no longer 'miserable', it 'stinks'.

U don't have a 'great' time, U have a 'ball'.

U don't 'sweat it out', U 'work U'r butt off'.

Never 'post' a letter, always 'mail' it and 'glue' the stamps, don't 'stick' them.

U no longer live in 'flats', U live in 'apartments'.

U don't stand in a 'queue', you are in a 'line'.

U no longer 'like' something, U 'appreciate' it.

'#' is not 'hash', it's 'pound'.

U are not 'deaf', U have 'impaired hearing'.

U are not 'lunatic', U are just 'mentally challenged'.

U are not 'disgusting', U R 'sick'.

U can't get 'surprised', U get 'zapped'.

U don't 'schedule' a meeting, U 'skejule' it.

U never 'joke', U just 'kid'.

U never 'increase' the pressure, U always 'crank' it up.

U don't try to find a lift... U find an elevator.

U no more ask for a route but for a 'RAUT'

U don't ask somebody 'How r u ?', U say, 'What's up dude?' or U say, 'How U DOIN'?

'U never go to see a game U go to watch a game'.

If U see 'World' champions (or Series), read 'USA' champions, (or Series).

There's no 'zero' but 'O', no 'Z' but 'zee'.

There's no FULL STOP after a statement, there's a PERIOD.

If someone gets angry at U, U get 'flamed'.

U Drive your car on Parkways and always park your car in the Drive-Way!

You do not ask for brinjal ... ask for an Egg-Plant...also there are no lady's finger...its Okra!

You do not say, 'He is a trouble creator' ... rather u say, 'He's a pain in my ass'!

U do not say... Its a trivial job... U say it's a seat of the pants work.

Well, U don't say life is boring, u say LIFE SUCKS!!!!!

In short, U don't speak English, U speak American.

f) Interpersonal skills

➤ *A man hooked a large fish. When someone enquired him whether he caught that large a fish all alone, his reply was, "No. Not alone. I had a small worm to help me."*

No one is an island. You will need the help of others —you will need to give help to others. To have a friend, be a friend. People, who cannot get along with others, will never get ahead in life. It is difficult to achieve success without the friendly cooperation of others. If you want to be successful, focus on people. Become genuinely interested in people. Try teamwork.

> **The law of network:** "The more people you know and who know you in a positive way, the luckier you will be. If people like you, they will give you ideas and open doors for you."

Make a new friend or acquaintance everyday. Keep an updated list of all contacts close at hand. Rich relationships are the DNA of a rich, rewarding life. Become a committed and sincere networker. Cultivate new friendships. You will truly be surprised where people end up over the years and how these small, kind gestures will help you later on in life. Treat everyone who crosses your path as if they are the most important person in your world. You will certainly meet with great success.

Get to know and enjoy your ***neighbours***. They make life more pleasant and can provide helpful resources when you least expect it.

People who have no friends are not the people who cannot make friends, but those who cannot keep them. 'To frighten a bird is not the way to catch it.' Replace **friction** with **harmony.**

Key to happy relationships

> **The law of happy relationships:** "People don't change, so deal with them as they are. Don't try to change others or expect them to change. What you see, is what you get. Unconditional acceptance of others is the key to happy relationships."

1) Never demand or threaten.
2) Always be friendly, gentle, courteous and patient.
3) Be tender with the young, compassionate with the aged, sympathetic with the striving and tolerant with the weak and strong.
4) Hold out your hand of friendship—offering something the other wants.
5) Never ridicule, nag or shout at anyone.
6) Share praise, but shoulder blame.
7) Don't be sarcastic.
8) Show concern for others. Be considerate.
9) Forgive and forget. Don't harbour resentment.
10) Practise humility.
11) In the science of human relations, tact takes first place. Tact is the essence of co-operative and productive activity. **Talent** is important but **Tact** is essential—

(i) Never tell a man, he is wrong. Show respect for other person's opinions.

(ii) Avoid arguments. Arguments are to prove who is right but not what is right.

(iii) Don't criticize, condemn or complain.

12) If you are wrong, admit it quickly.

13) Be genuine. Practise honesty, integrity and sincerity.

14) Accept responsibility and accountability.

15) In order to accumulate an abundance of good will, people must be influenced with—

Honest and sincere appreciation, Gratitude (thankful to others), Empathy (place yourself in other's shoes), Admiration, Cooperation, Friendship and Their desire for their own personal gain.

16) A) Fulfil the 'eager wants' of everyone—

To be appreciated, To feel important and To feel needed.

B) Remember everyone's name—

➤ *Napoleon III of France had a special ability to remember the names of those, he met. His secret was to say "so sorry, I missed your name", after being introduced to a new person. This would cause the name to be repeated and reinforced within his memory. If the name was difficult, he would ask for the proper spelling.*

Remember people's names and treat everyone well. This habit, along with enthusiasm, is one of the greatest success secrets. Everyone in this world wears an imaginary button that screams out "I WANT TO FEEL IMPORTANT AND APPRECIATED!"

17) Listen to people. **Interpersonal skill is essentially a skill in communication.**

18) Have a sense of humour.

19) Be likeable. Smile.

20) Be enthusiastic. Enthusiasm turns mediocrity to excellence.

21) Develop dependability. Confidence begets confidence. If you have confidence in yourself, others will believe you.

22) Commit to your promises and values.

23) Do more than is expected, before it is expected.

24) Think win-win.

25) Derive happiness in creating happiness for others.

➤ *Thomas Edison had at the entrance of his home a turnstile (big, clumsy gate). People often wondered why Edison liked this ugly gate. One day, Edison's friend tactfully asked him the secret behind this gate. Edison said, "Come, let me show you something."*

He went ahead and showed how the ugly gate, with the help of many pulleys and ropes, was used as a pumping device to fill his water tank. Edison remarked, "Every man who comes to see me, no matter who he is, automatically pumps a gallon of water into my water tank."

Why don't we also pick up a leaf out of Edison's life and learn to use people constructively? Let's start seeing in people their hidden potential.

Be soft as a flower, when it comes to kindness but tough as thunder, when it comes to principle. Be courteous and polite at all times but never be pushed around. Ensure that you are always treated with respect.

Associate only with positive, focused people who you can learn from and who will not drain your valuable energy with complaining and uninspiring attitudes. By developing relationships with those committed to constant improvement and the pursuit of the best that life has to offer, you will have plenty of company on your path to the top of whatever mountain you seek to climb.

g) Negotiation skills

Negotiation is a means to discuss, to communicate, and to interact with another human being in order to find a way to reach an agreement. The rules of negotiation are based on the principles of communication and cooperation. In negotiation, three basic aspects are involved—

- i) You,
- ii) The client/customer or whoever is to be negotiated with, and
- iii) Whatever being negotiated.

Each aspect is equal in the process of negotiation. All the three aspects must win. No one loses.

Rules: Listen to what the other person is saying. Stick to the subject. Never trample on the other person's ego. Sidestep any attempt by the other person to belittle you. Be prepared to give some concessions. Under no circumstances, give away something that is absolutely essential to you. **There is no such thing as winning an argument. There is only winning an agreement.**

Remember:

- ✓ Everything is negotiable.
- ✓ Always ask for more than you want.
- ✓ In business, you don't get what you deserve, you get what you negotiate.
- ✓ Timing is a critical aspect of any negotiation. Whenever you make an offer, give a deadline for acceptance.
- ✓ Before negotiating, be sure to get the facts, do your homework and check your assumptions.
- ✓ The one who wants the negotiation to succeed the most, has the least bargaining power.

h) Selling skills

Three things move the world:

IDEAS + MAKING THEM WORK + MAKING OTHERS LIKE THEM.

We are all salesmen, selling something or other—a service, an idea, a philosophy, or just ourselves. A young man applying for a job is selling his abilities; a lawyer, his legal skills; the stockbroker, his investment expertise; a priest, his faith; the politician, his party's idealism; a film star, his good looks and talent, etc.

Salesmanship is the art of converting people to one's own way of thinking. Some knowledge of salesmanship is important for everyone. Everyone needs it to become successful in his line of activity. Some people are better at it than others. They are the super salesmen, such as, Abraham Lincoln, Gandhi, Lenin, Hitler, Adnan Kashoggi and many more.

Salesmen are not born—they are made. A salesperson should possess certain qualities like—knowledge of his products/service/concept which he wants to sell, positive attitude, skills of presentation and motivation and habits that go to increase his ability.

You don't sell a *thing*; you sell the *benefits of a thing*.

There are millions of telephones sold each year. No one wants a telephone, but everyone wants the means of keeping an easy touch with others. Your needs are not important; customer's needs are. 'Sell the sizzle, not the steak.' *It is the sizzle that makes people's mouth water*.

Here is an advertising expert's checklist guide to the buying motives/impulses, what people want and the advantages, they are most interested in gaining.

PEOPLE WANT

Better health	To be good parents.
More money	To have influence on others.
Greater popularity	To be sociable and hospitable.
Improved appearance	To be gregarious.
Security in old age	To express their personalities.
Praise from others/vanity	To resist domination by others.
More comfort/Convenience	To satisfy their curiosity.
Gain	To achieve an ambition.
More leisure	To be up-to-date.
Pride of accomplishment	To emulate the admirable.
Business advancement	To appreciate beauty.
Social advancement/Prestige and status/self-respect	To be proud of their possessions/ownership.
Increase enjoyment from food, drink, entertainment, etc./Pleasure	To be creative.
Self-preservation	Love of family.
To acquire or collect things	To be efficient.
To win others' affection	To be 'first' in things.
To improve themselves mentally	To be recognised as authorities.
To save money and time	To work.
To avoid discomfort, risks, worry, doubts, offence to others, boredom, loss, embarrassment.	*Self-improvement.*

One of the above would be the basic appeal of any sale, either sale of a bar soap or a jumbo jet. The trick is to discover which of these is *dominant* in any particular situation. Forget about your own tastes and preferences; they are immaterial. Your job is to establish what the prospect wants, reinforce his desires and convince him/her that you have the best solution. **Then, you can sell a fridge, even to an Eskimo.**

'AIDCA' — The 5 stages in a successful sale are:

Attracting ATTENTION to win the customer's eyes and ears.

Developing INTEREST to set up the customer to be receptive to further information.

Inspiring DESIRE with embellishments in addition to the basic need.

Creating CONVICTION by presenting the unique selling proposition.

Inciting ACTION to make the customer place the order immediately by creating the elements of immediacy and urgency.

6th Rule

Direction giving **SELF-DISCIPLINE** (restraint/self-control/willpower/focus/concentration)

"Is not that a great principle for all of living? The people who will really accomplish great things in life are those who are willing to discipline their lives, who maintain their health, their vitality, their efficiency through this process of rigorous disciplining of what they take into their bodies and what they do in life. It's a very important thing in terms of championship living."

—Bob Richards,
Olympic Pole Vaulting Champion

Just as valuable energy is wasted by spending time on activities that are of no value. Similarly, energy can be wasted on loose thinking. Imagine that your mind has an energy measure of 1000 watts at its disposal. Each time your mind wanders off the project at hand, to a nagging worry, to all the things to do by the end of the day, 100 watts is lost. Quite soon, the entire energy supply is gone. This is the nature of the mind. Fail to discipline it, and your energy levels will be depleted and your accomplishments will be minimal.

Control it, and you will see great things happening. You will feel more powerful and achieve difficult tasks with ease. The 19th century philosopher, Henri Frederic Amiel summed it up nicely: "For purposes of action, nothing is more useful than narrowness of thought combined with energy of will."

➤ *A fat/obese person consulted a dietician for his weight problem. The dietician said, "There is a simple exercise for losing weight. Just turn your head from left to right." The obese person exclaimed, "That simple an exercise!" The dietician clarified, "This exercise is to be done, whenever you sit at the dining table." Nodding the head left to right, means to say 'no' to food. Is it that easy? It requires a lot of will power.*

One may argue that it is natural to enjoy food. How can the taste buds be restrained? Very true! To have a slim figure, one has to abstain from tempting sweets, savouries and other high calorie foods. Achievements are possible, only when natural instincts are curbed or restrained and harnessed by will power. There is no success without sacrifice.

➤ *It is natural for water to flow in all directions. When the same body of water is restrained by banks on either side, it gets momentum and moves in one direction. If a further restraint called a dam is constructed in front of it in its way, its power is harnessed to produce power to illuminate thousands of houses as well as to run various mills.*

The human mind, too has a tendency to wander in different directions. Such dissipations may be hindering our efforts in attaining our chosen goal. But the will power within us will focus our undivided attention to one thing at a time.

You must be able to control your mind so that you can make it to do what you want to do. Be willing to sacrifice pleasure for opportunity. 'Pay now, play later.' **For everything in life, you pay a price.** Only that can make a giant of you. Much of the first half of life is spent paying the price for later success. The greater dues you pay now, the more they compound, and the greater potential for a successful second half.

> ***The law of time preference:*** "You are impatient in virtually every area of your life. You always prefer earlier rather than later in the satisfaction of any desire."

Will Power: Enhance your will-power; it is likely one of the best training programs, you can invest in.

Will power is—

a) The relentless, driving, irresistible determination to obtain what you want, to reach a desired goal regardless of everything and

b) The willingness to pay the price—in sacrifice, in money, in time, in effort, in anyway in which the price of success must be paid.

A simple way to develop will power is to learn to say, 'No' to many things that offer pleasure, but come in the way of your attaining the chosen goal.

> **The law of direction/self discipline**: "Successful people have a clear sense of purpose and direction in every area of

their lives. Achievements are possible only when natural instincts are curbed or restrained and harnessed by will power. There is no success without sacrifice."

Here are some ideas to strengthen your will and become a stronger person:

a) Do not let your mind float like a piece of paper in the wind. Work hard to keep it focused at all times. When doing a task, think of nothing else. When walking to work, count the steps that it takes to get all the way to the office. This is not easy, but your mind will soon understand that you hold its reins and not vice versa. Your mind must, eventually become as still as a candle flame in a corner where there is no draft.

b) Your will is like a muscle. You must first exercise it and then push before it gets stronger. This necessarily involves short term pain, but be assured that the improvements will come and will touch your character in a most positive way. When you are hungry, wait for another hour before your meal. When you are labouring over a difficult task and your mind is prompting you to pick up the latest magazine for a break or to get up and go talk to a friend, curb the impulse. Soon, you will be able to sit for hours in a precisely concentrated state. Sir Isaac Newton, one of the greatest classical physicists, the world has ever produced, once said: "If I have done the public any service, it is due to patient thought." Newton had a remarkable ability to sit quietly and think without interruption for very long periods of time. If he can develop this so can you.

c) You can also build your willpower by restraint in your conduct with others. Speak less (use the 60/40 Rule = listen 60% of the time and speak a mere 40%). This will not only make you more popular but you will learn much wisdom as everyone we meet everyday, has something to teach us. Also, restrain the urge to gossip or to condemn someone who you feel has made a mistake. Stop complaining and develop a cheerful, vital and strong personality. You will greatly influence others.

d) When a negative thought comes to your mind, immediately replace it with one that is positive. Positive always dominates over the negative and your mind has to be conditioned to think only the best thoughts. Negative thinking is a conditioned process whereby the negative patterns are established over and over. Rid yourself of any limitations and become a powerful positive thinker.

✓ *Willingness opens the doors to knowledge, direction and achievement. Be willing to know, be willing to do, be willing to create a positive result. Be willing, especially, to follow your dream.*

Push yourself just a little harder and a little farther each day. Winners on the playing field of life, push the envelope of their potential, daily. Do the thing you fear, and the death of fear is certain. Winners do the things that less developed people don't like doing even though they also might not enjoy doing them. This is what strength of character and courage is all about. Tackle your weaknesses. Do the thing that you have consistently put off. Write that 'thank you note' or letter that you have neglected for so long. Exercise your discipline muscles and they will rise to the occasion by filling your day with more satisfaction, effectiveness and far more energy.

7th Rule

Massive, positive, constructive and consistent **ACTION** with flexibility in pursuing goals (sustained effort/ hard work/act aggressively and boldly/ commitment to action/work with dedication/high endeavour/ toil/just do it/diligence)

The law of applied effort

"All your hopes, dreams, goals and aspirations are amenable to hard work. The harder you work, the luckier you get. There are no shortcuts."

The law of compensation

"The universe is completely balanced and in perfect order. You will always be compensated in full for everything you do. You will get out what you put in."

Wishes are like dreams for they don't come true unless we do something about it. **Wishbones satisfy dreamers where as doers put backbone into the wish and make their dreams come true.** The Chinese proverb says, "Great souls have wills; feeble ones have only wishes."

➤ The Race at Sunrise

Every morning in Africa, A gazelle wakes up. It knows that it must run faster than the fastest lion, or it will be killed. Every morning, a lion wakes up. It knows that it must outrun the slowest gazelle, or it will starve to death. It doesn't matter whether you are a lion or a gazelle: When the sun comes up, you had better be running.

Human effort is a significant component in the success of any venture. **Action produces achievement for achievement is success.** Enthusiasm is the lubricant that oils the machinery of action. It is the passion/enthusiasm that drives us towards our goals, but it is the hard work that yields success. Action requires courage. Action also develops courage.

Never confuse **motion** with **action.**

Your success is assured, if you will devote to doing everything, you should do.

Make yourself do the thing—

1) You should do
2) When it is ought to be done and
3) Whether you like it not.

The man who gets ahead, is the one who does more than necessary and keeps on doing it.

Fill your day with **accomplishments** and not mere **activities.**

8th Rule

PERSISTENCE (perseverance/tenacity of purpose/fantastic determination/press on/ never give up/never-say-die attitude/ stick-to-it/endurance/patience)

Success is the result of planning, patience and perseverance. Success always comes to those, who try hard and long enough. **The life of successful men is not a story of continuous successes.** Read the following list of failures, in a span of 30 years, predominating the life of one of the greatest personalities of all time.

➤ *He failed in his business in 1831.*

He failed in his first step at politics, when he was defeated for the legislature in 1832.

His sweetheart died in 1835.

He had a nervous breakdown in 1836.

He was defeated for the elector in 1840.

He was defeated in his first attempt to be nominated for the congress in 1843.

He was defeated in his aspirations to be the commissioner of the General land office.

He was defeated for the congress in 1848.

He was defeated in the senatorial election in 1854.

He was defeated in his attempt to become the vice president in 1856.

He was again defeated in the senatorial election in 1858.

He was elected the President of United States in 1860.

Do you know, who this great gentleman is? It's ABRAHAM LINCOLN!

How many of us would have survived such a litany of failures. He had the courage not to allow defeat to get him down. Failures toughen a person as well as bring out his inner reserve of strength.

In the struggle for existence, the fittest only survives. Persistence produces power. To fail proves, you are trying. Every failure is a dress rehearsal for success. Every opportunity for success also contains the possibility for failure. Never, never, never give up. The words failure and defeat are not the same. **Failure is simply a step towards success.** So 'Fail forward'.

Never consider defeat and remove from your vocabulary such words as quit, cannot, unable, impossible, failure, unworkable, hopeless and retreat, for they are the words of fools.

With ordinary talent and extraordinary perseverance, all things are attainable. **Winners never quit, and quitters never win.** When you get to the end of a rope, tie a knot and hang on.

➤ **Ernest Hemingway**: Persevered with 'The old man and the sea' and reviewed his manuscript eighty times.

Gibbon: Persevered for twenty-six long years to complete—'The Decline and fall of the Roman Empire'.

Leonardo da Vinci: Persevered for ten years in perfecting his painting—'The last supper'.

Michelangelo: Persevered for eight years to complete his painting—'The last judgement'.

Milton: Persevered every morning from 4 a.m. to write—'Paradise Lost'.

Noah Webster: After 36 years of perseverance was able to compile—Webster's Dictionary.

Don't quit

When things go wrong, as they sometimes will,
Then the road you're trudging seems all uphill,
When the funds are low and the debts are high,
And you want to smile, but you have to sigh,
When care is pressing you down a bit,
Rest, you must—but don't you quit,
Life is queer with its twists and turns,
As everyone of us sometimes learns,
And many a failure turns about,
When he might have won had he stuck it out,
Don't give up, though the pace seems slow,
You might succeed with another blow,

Success is failure turned inside out, the silver tint of the clouds of doubt,

And you never can tell how close you are, it may be near when it seems so far,

So, stick to the fight when you're hardest hit,

It's when things seem worst, that you MUST NOT QUIT!

9th Rule

PRAYERS (God+you = synergy)

Mahatma Gandhi brought down the British Empire, with no resources like capital or military force but only with lived values and soul power. He, who mobilized the 400 million Indians to bring down the British Empire, was inspired by the 'Sermon on the Mount' and 'Bhagavad Gita'. He derived his great strength from his ardent faith in God and his regular prayer.

- *All living things have the same element—**Soul,** interconnecting them like the common thread of a garland with flowers of different hues, colours, fragrance, shapes and sizes. All these souls are connected or part of that, **the Universal Soul, we call God.** Connect yourself to that Universal Source through prayer and meditation to draw power to strengthen your inner self. As you charge your cell phone regularly, you shall charge your soul from the universal soul through prayer.*
- **The partnership with God:**

  One self-made man, who rose from rags to riches, when enquired by a reporter, revealed the secret of his success as follows—"The secret of my success is indeed very simple. I have a partnership with God. I do the work myself and leave the anxiety to my partner. That is how our partnership goes on."

➤ **Work with commitment towards the goal.**

Make it a mission. Don't settle for less than your best. Do your best and let God do the rest. When you know you have done all that is possible with love in any situation, then the problem is no longer yours. When we do everything from heart with happiness and devotion, our work becomes worship/prayer and an offering at the altar.

➤ **Work and Prayer:**

A boatman painted his oars with the words, Prayer and Work. When he was asked for the reason, he replied by taking hold of the first oar marked, Prayer, and pulling on it. "You see," he explained, "when I use only Prayer, the boat spins round in circle and we make no progress at all." Then, he took hold of the second oar marked, Work and pulled on that. "The same result", he remarked. He finally, took one oar in each hand and got into a steady pull. "Prayer and Work must pull together," he added with a smile as the boat shot rapidly across the stream.

The answer to your **prayer** is not according to your faith while you only talk, but according to your faith when you **Work.** Efficiency experts use the words, **wishing** and **willing** in place of **prayer** and **work.** *Wishes are like dreams; they don't come true unless we do something about it.*

➤ **Once you get going, the going gets easier:**

Once, a successful person was asked about the secret of his success. He revealed that the secret of success was given to him when he visited the famous South Indian Balaji temple in Tirumala Tirupathi. In the long, crowded queue, when he reached the sanctum sanctorum, and he hardly had the glimpse of the deity, he heard the priests shouting, "Keep moving, keep moving". He took it as a dictum from God and was obliged. He kept on moving to attain this stage of great success.

Remember—**the power of prayer.**

10th Rule

VALUES/Virtues/Ethics/Character/Integrity

Values are organising factors within the personality that are related to morals and characters. Values influence the attitudes, perception, needs and motives of people. Values are the basis of human behaviour. Values are so much couched in the personalities of the individuals that they can be perceived in the form of attitudes and behaviour.

Character has to be built with all the virtues of life cultivating the soul. A person who operates from knowledge, (acquired from outside through media like books, T.V, news and external experience) always depends on other people and circumstances for his happiness. A person with wisdom, (realisation achieved from within through experience and reflection) always carries happiness with him. Actually, what we get from outside is only pleasure, whereas what lies within us is happiness. Learn to live with values and wisdom to look within for happiness.

Contentment comes from within. 'Guard your heart more than any treasure for it is the source of all life.'

We should never do things against our conscience for an act which is done against the conscience, leads to stress. To lead a stressless life, one should go with the conscience, not against it.

One has to learn to live life by adding life to years, not just years to life. We make a living by what we get but we make a life by what we give. **No person was ever honoured for what he received. Honour has been the reward for what he gave.**

➤ *Here is the story of eight men who knew how to make money. In 1923, these eight wealthy men met in Chicago. Among them, was the president of the largest steel company, the head of the largest utility company, the greatest wheat speculator, the president of the New York Stock Exchange, the president of the Bank of International Settlements, a member of the president's cabinet, the greatest man in New York Wall Street and the head of the largest monopoly.*

Twenty five years later: The president of the largest steel company, *Charles Schwab,* died a bankrupt.

The head of the largest utility company, *Samuel Insull,* died a fugitive from justice, an exile in Greece.

The greatest wheat speculator, *Arthur Cuttin,* died abroad insolvent.

The president of the New York Stock Exchange, *Richard Whitney,* served time in Sing Sing prison.

The president of the Bank of International Settlements, *Leon Fraser,* committed suicide.

The member of the president's cabinet, *Albert Fall,* was released from prison so he could die at his home.

The greatest man in New York Wall Street, *Jesse Livermore,* committed suicide.

The head of the largest monopoly, *Ivan Kruger,* the match king, committed suicide.

All these men knew well how to make money, but they never learned how to live. Choosing a balance between earning and spending, enriches life.

For attaining stability in life, the following five areas in our life, require balancing—

1. Faith 2. Family 3. Fitness 4. Friends 5. Finances.

Faith: Faith forms the core and the other four 'Fs' are balanced by it. In the core, if faith is weak or missing, the other four 'Fs'—Family, Fitness, Friends and Finances, collapse from even the slightest pressure. Connect yourself to that Universal Source, called God, through prayer and meditation to draw power to strengthen your inner self.

Family: Be close to your family. You owe your parents your love, respect and kindness; your children, your quality time, etc. Don't take your family for granted and ignore them. A strong family is a key ingredient to a balanced life. Without love and affection, life will be dreary.

Fitness: When you have got your health, you have got everything. Keep your body fit. Remember—no **health, no energy.** No energy, no accomplishments/ no enjoyments.

Friends: Friends balance your life and keep you on an even keel. **You cannot choose your relatives, but you can choose your friends.** It is a matter of choice, not chance.

Finances: Money itself has no value, but what money can buy has value to us. Money gives us freedom—freedom from hunger, tedious chores, getting treatments done, sending children to lousy schools, freedom to make your own choices, to do what you want to do, etc.

In the above narrated story about the eight men, all the eight died unhappy, broke, and in disgrace. All these men learned well how to make money, but they never learned the value of balance. Hence, **balance in life is very essential.**

➤ Emperor and the seed that didn't grow!

An emperor in the Far East was growing old and knew it was time to choose his successor. Instead of choosing one of his assistants or his children, he decided something different. He called all the young people in the kingdom together, one day. He said, "It is time for me to step down and choose the next emperor. I have decided to choose one of you." The children were shocked! But, the emperor continued. "I am going to give each one of you a seed today, one very special seed. I want you to plant the seed, water it and come back here one year from today with what you have grown from this one seed. I will then judge the plants that you bring, and the one I choose will be the next emperor!"

One boy, named Ling was there that day and he, like the others, received a seed. He went home and excitedly told his mother the story. She, helped him get a pot and planting soil, and he planted the seed and watered it carefully. Everyday, he would water it and watch to see if it had grown.

After about three weeks, some of the other youths began to talk about their seeds and the plants that were beginning to grow. Ling, kept checking his seed, but nothing ever grew. Three weeks, 4 weeks, 5 weeks went by. Still, nothing had happened. By now, others were talking about their plants, but Ling didn't have a plant, and he felt like a failure. Six months went by, still nothing in Ling's pot. Everyone else had trees and tall plants, but he had nothing. Ling didn't say anything to his friends, however. He just kept waiting for his seed to grow.

A year, finally went by and all the youths of the kingdom brought their plants to the emperor for inspection. Ling, told his mother that he wasn't going to take an empty pot and will be honest about what happened. He knew his mother was right. But he took his empty pot to the palace. When Ling arrived, he was amazed at the variety of plants grown by the other youths. They were beautiful, in all shapes and sizes. Ling put his empty pot on the floor and many of the other youths laughed at him. A few felt sorry for him and just said, "Hey nice try."

When the emperor arrived, he surveyed the room and greeted the young people.

Ling just tried to hide in the back. "My, what great plants, trees and flowers you have grown," said the emperor. "Today, one of you will be appointed the next emperor!" All of a sudden, the emperor spotted Ling at the back of the room with his empty pot. He ordered his guards to bring him to the front. Ling was terrified and thought, "The emperor knows I'm a failure! Maybe, he will have me killed!" When Ling got to the front, the emperor, asked his name. "My name is Ling," he replied. All the kids were laughing and making fun of him.

The emperor asked everyone to keep quiet. He looked at Ling, and then announced to the crowd, "Behold your new emperor! His name is Ling!" Ling couldn't believe it.

Ling couldn't even grow his seed. How could he be the new emperor? Asked the gathered youths. Then the emperor said, "One year ago today, I gave everyone here a seed. I told you to take the seed, plant it, water it, and bring it back to me today. But I gave you all ***boiled seeds*** *which* ***would not grow****. All of you, except Ling, have brought me trees and plants and flowers. When you found that the seed would not grow, you substituted another seed for the one I gave you. Ling, was the only one with the* ***courage and honesty*** *to bring me a pot with my seed in it. Therefore, he is the one who will be the new* ***emperor!"***

If you plant honesty, you will reap trust.
If you plant goodness, you will reap friends.
If you plant humility, you will reap greatness.
If you plant perseverance, you will reap victory.
If you plant consideration, you will reap harmony.
If you plant hard work, you will reap success.
If you plant forgiveness, you will reap reconciliation.

If you plant openness, you will reap intimacy.
If you plant patience, you will reap improvements.
If you plant faith, you will reap miracles.

So, be careful what you plant now, it will determine what you will reap tomorrow. The seeds you sow will make life worse or better for you. Someday, you will enjoy the fruits, or you will pay for the choices you plant today.

It has been rightly said that "you sow an action, you reap a habit. You sow a habit, you reap a character. You sow a character, you reap a destiny." The essence of a person is his character. So make yours unique, unblemished and strong.

- The golden rule your parents and your kindergarten teacher taught you was pretty simple:

  "Do unto others as you'd have others do unto you." Imagine, how you'd feel if you were in the other person's shoes.
- Stand up for yourself, but try not to hurt people's feelings.
- Do not say you will do anything unless you will indeed do it.
- Speak the truth and measure your words wisely.
- Be humble, straightforward and peaceful.
- **Each day, do two things that you do not like doing.** This may be the preparation of a report, you have been putting off or shining your shoes. It does not matter how small the task, just do it! Soon, these chores will not seem so bad, your personal power will increase and your

productivity will soar. Try it because this is an age-old technique for *building strength of character*.

- The sages of China, have held a basic life philosophy for thousands of years: "Develop an indomitable spirit along with courtesy and integrity." The repetition of these three traits will make you an exceptionally powerful individual respected by all. Exert your effort and personal influence to attain these qualities.
- Be the master of your will but the servant of your conscience.
- Be the most honest person.
- Be trustworthy—worthy of the trust of others.
- Sleep less, spend less, do more and live longer.

➤ **Benjamin Franklin's thirteen virtues:** *Benjamin Franklin, scientist, inventor, educator, diplomat, politician, statesman, philosopher and humorist, in his autobiography, assures you that by making a habit of the following thirteen virtues, success and happiness would always be with us. Just take one virtue at a time, master it and then proceed to another and so on, until you have gone through all thirteen of them. By the time, you have reached the last one, Franklin says, your life would not be the same.*

The 13 virtues with their precepts are:

1. **Temperance:** Eat not to dullness; drink not to elevation.
2. **Silence:** Speak not but what may benefit others or yourself. Avoid trifling conversation.

3. **Order:** Let all your things have their places. Let each part of your business have its time.
4. **Resolution:** Resolve to perform what you ought to and perform without fail what you resolve.
5. **Frugality:** Make no expense but to do good to others or yourself; i.e., waste nothing.
6. **Industry:** Lose no time. Be always busy, but cut all unnecessary actions.
7. **Sincerity:** Use no hurtful deceit. Think innocently and justly; and, if you speak, speak accordingly.
8. **Justice:** Wrong none by doing injuries or by omitting the benefits that are due to them.
9. **Moderation:** Avoid extremes. Forbear resenting injuries so much as you think they deserve.
10. **Cleanliness:** Tolerate no uncleanness in body, clothes or habitation.
11. **Tranquillity:** Be not disturbed at trifles or at accidents common or unavoidable.
12. **Chastity:** Rarely use venery but for health or offspring—never to dullness, weakness, or the injury of your own or another's peace or reputation.
13. **Humility:** Imitate Jesus and Socrates.

Character has to be built with all the virtues of life cultivating the soul.

Virtue Capsules

✓ The paradox of our time in history is that —

We have taller buildings, but shorter tempers; Wider freeways, but narrower viewpoints;

We spend more, but have less;

We buy more, but enjoy less;

We have multiplied possessions, but reduced our values.

We talk too much, love seldom and hate too often.

We've learned how to make a living, but not a life;

We've added years to life, not life to years.

We've been all the way to the moon and back, but have trouble crossing the street to meet the new neighbour.

We've conquered outer space, but not inner space;

We've cleaned up the air, but polluted the soul;

We've slit the atom, but not our prejudice.

We have higher incomes, but lower morals;

We've become long on quantity, but short on quality.

These are times of tall men and short character; Steep profits and shallow relationships..

✓ 21st CENTURY ... USELESS!!!???

>Our communication – Wireless

>Our dress – Topless

>Our telephone – Cordless

>Our cooking – Fireless

>Our youth – Jobless

>Our religion – Creedless

>Our food – Fatless

>Our labour – Effortless

>Our conduct – Worthless

>Our relation – Loveless

>Our attitude – Careless

>Our feelings – Heartless

>Our politics – Shameless

>Our education – Valueless

>Our follies – Countless

>Our arguments – Baseless

>Our faith – Godless

✓ **Do all the good,** you can,

by all the means, you can,

in all the ways, you can,

in all the places, you can,

at all the times, you can,

to all the people, you can, and

as long as ever, you can.

✓ Heart is like a crystal.... Preserve it. Love is like perfume... spread it. Feelings are like flood.... Flow it. Friendship is like an umbrella.... Share it.

✓ Simplify your **wants,**

Nullify your **greed,**

Amplify your **work,**

Rectify your **mistakes,**

Justify your **expenses,**

Certify your **conduct,**

Magnify your **mind,**

Glorify your **future,**

Think big. Talk small,

Love much. **Laugh** easily,

Work happily. **Play** fair,

Pay cash, and **be kind**.

✓ Do More

DO MORE THAN...

Exist: **Live**.	Hear: **Listen.**
Touch: **Feel**	Listen: **Understand**.
Look: **Observe**.	Think: **Reflect**.
Read: **Absorb**.	Just talk: **Say something**.

✓ Twelve things to remember:

1. The value of **time**.
2. The success of **perseverance.**
3. The pleasure of **working.**
4. The dignity of **simplicity**.
5. The worth of **character.**
6. The power of **kindness**.
7. The influence of **example**.
8. The obligation of **duty.**
9. The wisdom of **economy**.
10. The virtue of **patience.**
11. The improvement of **talent**.
12. The joy of **originating.**

'You Company'.

That is all about the ten keys that open the lock called success.

You are the chairman of the company— *'You Company.'* and are in full control of the same. You are 100% responsible for the performance of 'YOU Company.' Personal success is your personal responsibility. Being in control, means taking responsibility for your performance and monitoring your progress.

You must develop yourself by working on yourself. Read the positive books. A number of titles are available on self-development/self-help/success. If you want to know more in detail about success methods, you can read such self-help/inspirational books. The titles, '50 Self-help classics' and '50 Success classics' (by Tom Butler Bowdon, Nicholas Brealey Publishing, London, 2003) and another title, 'Read & grow rich' (by Burke Hedges, INTI Publishing, USA) provide a very good introduction to some of the important self-help classics.

Get into the excellent habit of reading something positive and inspirational before you go to bed and as soon as you are awake in the morning. You will soon note the benefits as these thoughts will be supporting you throughout the day.

Become a committed audio-tape/CD user. Most self-mastery programs and books are now offered in this format. Listen to these inspirational materials on your way to work, whilst waiting in the line at a bank or while you wash dishes in the evening. Make your car a college on wheels and use the drive time to make knowledge your best friend. All down time can be very effectively used in this productive fashion. Use such opportunities to learn and continually expand your mind and its vast potential.

Do not take personal development books as gospel. Read them and take whatever useful ideas you need. Some people feel they must do everything suggested and take the techniques to extremes. Every book has at least one tool or strategy of benefit. Take what you need and what works for you and discard what doesn't suit you.

Success (soft/life) skills such as effective communication, effective presentations, leadership, critical thinking, creative thinking, decision making, problem solving, change management, achieving self-confidence, interpersonal relationship, coping with emotions and stress, self awareness, memory skills, continuous improvement, selling, negotiating, etc. are not taught, either in schools or in colleges.

Skills can be acquired by training

a) There are many motivational speakers/ academies, who/which train people in the aforesaid skills.['Ace Training Foundation', 'Achiever's Centre', 'Career Care', 'Life Academy', 'MAX', 'MILT', 'MTS Academy', 'Oneiric', 'Only

Success', 'Prerana Educational Media Private Ltd.', 'Ramanathans', 'Speak 2 Achieve', 'VETA', 'Winner's Choice', 'ZEAL', etc are some of such institutes conducting personal development seminars/training courses in Chennai (India). Such academies may also be found in your area.]

b) There are also a number of sites (www.freeskills.com, etc) on the web where such courses are available.

Avail yourself of the training opportunities available with them to acquire the success skills and achieve success. Best of luck!

To The Reader, I Wish

Addition to your friends,
Subtraction from wants,
Multiplication of your blessings,
Division among your foes.

Bibliography

- Anant Pai, 'How to achieve success', UBSPD, New Delhi, 1992.
- AP Pereira, 'Success in 30 days', Better Yourself Books, Mumbai, 1994.
- Atul John Rego, 'How to develop a pleasing personality', Better Yourself Books, Mumbai, 2000.
- Brian Tracy, 'The 100 absolutely unbreakable laws of business success', Magna Publishing Co. Ltd., Mumbai, 2001.
- Burke Hedges, 'Read & grow rich', INTI Publishing, USA.
- Burke Hedges, 'You, Inc.', INTI Publishing, USA, 1996.
- Dr. Chan Teng Heng, 'Access the minds of CEOs', Times Books International, Singapore, 2000.
- C N N Rao, 'The secret of success in life', Chadaram Book Trust, Secunderabad, 1997.
- Connie Palladino, Ph.D., 'Developing Self-Esteem', Viva Books Pvt. Ltd., New Delhi, 2004
- Denise Waitley & Reni L. Witt, 'The joy of working', Ballantine books, New York, 1986.
- Edwin C. Bliss, 'Getting things done', Bantam Books, USA, 1978.

- ESSEN, PhD, 'Especially for you', NR Publishing, Mumbai, 2001.
- Glenn J Cook, 'The art of making people listen to you', Tarang Paperbacks, a division of Vikas Publishing House Pvt Ltd, New Delhi, 1996.
- Greg Vance, 'Live a better life', Master Mind Books, Bangalore, 1999.
- Jeffrey J. Mayer, 'Success is a journey', Tata McGraw- Hill, New Delhi, 2003.
- John C. Maxwell, 'Success, one day at a time', Magna Publishing Co Pvt Ltd. Mumbai, 2003.
- Kate Keenan, "The Management guide to managing", Pustak Mahal, New Delhi, 2000.
- L.Jesse Lemisch-editor, 'Benjamin Franklin, The Autobiography And Other Writings', Signet Classic, New American Library, New York, USA, 1961.
- Marvelle S. Colby, "Test your management IQ", Pan Books Ltd, London, 1985.
- M.R.Kopmeyer, 'How to get whatever you want', UBSPD. New Delhi, 1994.
- M.R.Kopmeyer, 'How can you get richer ...quicker', UBSPD. New Delhi, 1994.
- Mack R. Douglas, 'How to make a habit of succeeding', UBSPD, New Delhi, 1995.
- Merril Douglass, 'Success secrets', Pustak Mahal, New Delhi, 2000.
- Michael Jeffreys, 'Success secrets of 15 motivational superstars', Jaico Publishing House, Mumbai, 2002.

- The Mothers' Department of the University Society, Inc, and USA, 'The Bookshelf Plan of Child Development', 1989.
- Tom Butler-Bowdon, '50 Self-help classics' Nicholas Brealey Publishing, London, 2003.
- Tom Butler-Bowdon, '50 Success classics' Nicholas Brealey Publishing, London, 2003.
- William Davis, 'The super salesman's handbook', Arrow Books, London, 1988.
- Willie Jolley, 'It only takes a minute to change your life', Master Mind Books, Bangalore, 2001.

■■

Career Management

visit our online bookstore:
www.vspublishers.com

Career Management

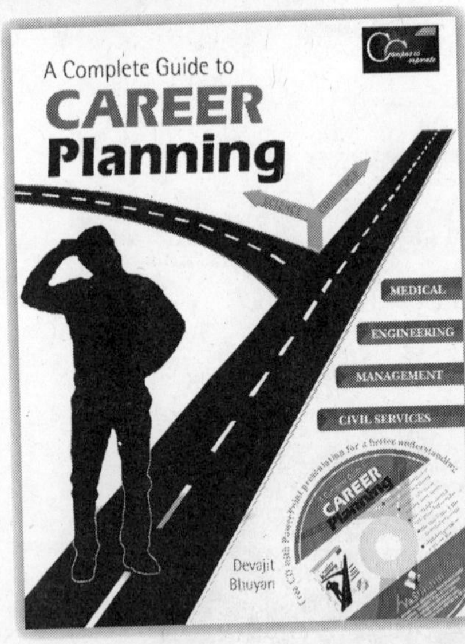

visit our online bookstore:
www.vspublishers.com

Career Management

visit our online bookstore:
www.vspublishers.com

Career Management

visit our online bookstore:
www.vspublishers.com